C For Yourself

For Yourself

Learning C Using Experiments

Richard P. Halpern
State University of New York—New Paltz

New York   Oxford
OXFORD UNIVERSITY PRESS
1997

OXFORD UNIVERSITY PRESS

Oxford   New York
Athens   Auckland   Bangkok   Bogotà   Bombay   Buenes Aires
Calcutta   Cape Town   Dar es Salaam   Delhi
Florence   Hong Kong   Istanbul   Karachi
Kuala Lumpur   Madras   Madrid   Melbourne
Mexico City   Nairobi   Paris   Singapore
Taipei   Tokyo   Toronto

and associated companies in

Berlin   Ibadan

Library of Congress Cataloging-in-Publication Data
Halpern, Richard P.
C for yourself : learning C using experiments /
Richard Halpern.
p.   cm.
Includes bibliographical references and index.
ISBN 0-19-510841-8 (pbk.)
1. C (Computer program language)
I. Title.
QA76.73.C15H34 1997
005.13'3—dc20   96-26967

Printing (last digit): 9 8 7 6 5 4 3 2

Printed in the United States of America
on acid-free paper

This book is dedicated to the memory of
Irving and Manya Halpern

"They shall obtain joy and gladness, and
sorrow and suffering shall flee away."

Johannes Brahms
"A German Requiem"

Contents

Preface

This book contains four types of material. Obviously, the lion's share of it is material that attempts to explain *C*. Periodically, though, these attempts cease, and you are asked to sit down at a computer for the purpose of testing out certain ideas. This happens at the places in the book labeled **Experiments**.[1] It is extremely important that you do them, since one of the goals of this book is to get you to figure things out on your own. Appendix A has "answers" to these, in case you run into a snag. (Of course, no one can stop you from simply looking at the answers, then continuing with the text. However, there's no substitute for the real thing. Actually *doing* something gives you a feel for the material that you can't get by simply reading.)

At the end of each section, there are **Exercises**. These are meant to be done with pencil and paper only. Many of them essentially ask that you go through a fragment of code the way a computer would. Like exercises in any walk of life, they can be boring. But you need to do enough of them to drill the specific ideas they represent into your head.

Finally, there are the **Programming Problems.** This is why you're studying *C* in the first place. For these, you obviously need a computer. But you need pencil and paper almost as much. Like any problem, a programming problem is best solved only *after* you have thought about it for a while and sketched out a solution on paper. If you had a dollar for every hour programmers have wasted because they started typing at the computer before thinking about a problem, you could retire (and not have to read this book). The **Programs** are found at the end of each chapter.

Good luck!

---

[1] Yes, you can experiment with computers all you want. They don't blow up.

1 The Basics

We begin our study of *C* by introducing many of its basic components: *identifiers, variables, symbolic constants, simple data types, operators, expressions*, and *statements*. These components are the building blocks of a *program*, which we can think of as a sequence of steps that the computer can carry out (*execute*). Periodically, we will need to represent the execution of a program pictorially. Figure 1.1 shows the scheme we will use; here, a sequence of upper-case letters represents the steps of the program. Execution starts with step A and proceeds downward in the diagram. Occasionally, a particular step will need some elaboration. In that case, we will use a rectangle (Figure 1.1b) or diamond (Figure 1.1c) to represent the step; details of the step will be given inside the rectangle/diamond.

We will illustrate the ideas presented in this chapter with two complete programs. The first is Program 1.1, which really does almost nothing. It is used merely to underscore the following three ideas about *C* programs:

- All *C* programs must have at least one section, called `main()`, along with a pair of braces (`{ }`) that mark the beginning and the end of the section. In Program 1.1, this structure is quite evident, as there is only one line of code between the braces.

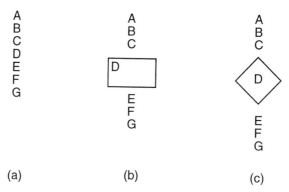

Figure 1.1   Possible symbolic diagrams for programs.

- A programmer can use indentation and spaces to make the program readable. Note, for example, that the section **main** is typed on four lines, two of which have only one character—a brace—on a line.
- Good *C* programs usually have *comments*. These explain to the reader what one or another part of the program is about. A comment begins with a "**/***" and ends with a "***/**". In Program 1.1, the comment tells the reader what will be printed out. Comments are ignored by the computer.

NOTE: The numbers at the left enclosed in square brackets in the example programs are not part of the program. They have been included in the examples for reference only.

Program 1.2, to which we will refer many times in this chapter, illustrates the basic program components referred to in the first paragraph of this section. This is a very simple program written for a hypothetical used car dealer who at one time lost a great deal of money when a storm damaged most of the vehicles on the lot. The dealer wishes to insure all cars and trucks in stock against possible future storm damage, and uses this program to calculate the cost. With the exception of a few details, we can get a good idea of what this program does from the program listing and the comments, even though we know little or nothing about *C* at this point.

1.1

IDENTIFIERS

We can immediately recognize some elements of Program 1.2 as familiar words: `cars`, `CREDIT`, `define`, `float`, `include`, `main`, `total`, and `trucks`. Other elements look almost recognizable: `CAR_RATE`, `printf`, and `TRUCK_RATE`. All these terms are formally called *identifiers*; they are simply names given to the elements of this program. The rules for constructing an identifier are simple:

1. The sequence must begin with a letter or the underscore character, _.
2. The remaining characters can be any combination of letters, digits, and the underscore.
3. Other characters are forbidden.

In *C*, everything we use must have a name!

Examples: **Valid and Invalid Identifiers**

Valid identifiers: temp, TEMP, f316x, Hi_There, _HiThere

Invalid identifiers: 5TEMP, Hi-There, F136*

C is case sensitive; upper- and lower-case versions of the same character are considered to be different. Hence `CAR_RATE` and `car_Rate` are two different identifiers.

A programmer has almost complete freedom to pick identifiers. We say "almost" because there are some identifiers that we can't use for our own purposes. In Program 1.2, these are `float` and `int`. They are examples of *keywords*, predefined terms with special meanings. A complete list of them is found in Appendix C. Since the choice is otherwise unlimited, it makes sense to use names that reasonably describe the quantity being represented. The identifier `CAR_RATE` is reasonably descriptive; the identifier `CR` is not.

Although legal, it is not a good idea to begin an identifier with the underscore character. This is because on many computer systems, variables that are used by the system software itself often begin with an underscore. (It makes such variables easily recognizable by systems personnel.) There is no point in risking confusion between variables we choose for our programs and the system variables.

1.2

SYMBOLIC CONSTANTS

A *symbolic constant*[1] is a quantity that has an unchanging value associated with it.

Examples: **Symbolic Constants**

In Program 1.2, `CAR_RATE`, whose value is `20.5`, `TRUCK_RATE`, whose value is `31`, and `CREDIT`, whose value is `-25`, are all symbolic constants.

Here is why constants are so important. Let us imagine that Program 1.2 really contains about a thousand lines of code, not a dozen, and that `CAR_RATE` and `TRUCK_RATE` appear many times throughout. It is reasonable to want to reuse the same program when the insurance rates change. If the two rates have names whose

---

1 For the sake of brevity, we'll call symbolic constants, simply, *constants*.

values are set in two lines at the beginning of the program, then changing the many occurrences of those rates is as simple as changing two lines. One need not search through a thousand lines of code to isolate the many instances of these values. Another reason why constants are valuable is this: not all occurrences of the numbers 20.5 and 31 necessarily represent insurance rates. For example, 31 might represent the days in a month. In that case, we would not wish to change that particular instance of the value 31 (a risk we would take if we used the search and replace feature of a word processor). By defining and using constants, we avoid these problems.

1.3

VARIABLES

We all have a mental picture of a *variable*—something that can take on different values—from our contact with ordinary algebra. In general, this view of a variable will not fail us. However, we need to add to it. To understand why, we must digress a little.

All computers need a place to store the information that they manipulate. That place is called the *memory*. Basically, we can think of memory as a huge quantity of tiny electronic storage compartments. To distinguish one compartment from another, each is identified by a unique integer called an *address*. In Figure 1.2, we have drawn a symbolic picture of a hypothetical memory with nine compartments. This is typical of the way we will picture a computer's memory. Each box represents one of these compartments; the numbers at the left denote the addresses of the compartments. (We'll discuss the names at the right shortly.) Sometimes the quantity to be stored at an address is small, so it can fit into a single compartment. Often, a quantity is larger,

Figure 1.2   Schematic diagram of a computer's memory.

0	
1	cars
2	
3	
4	trucks
5	
6	
7	
8	

so it requires a group of several adjacent compartments. We use the term *location* to refer to any combination of one or more compartments required to store a quantity.

Now let's get back to the main story. Every practical *C* program deals with quantities that change over the course of the program. Each such quantity is represented by a variable whose name is chosen by the programmer. For each variable name, the computer sets aside a unique location in the memory. The programmer deals only with the name; the computer takes care of finding its actual location. We can think of a variable, then, as a named location in memory. In Figure 1.2, `cars` and `trucks` are names for the locations `1` and `4`, respectively. Note that in an actual program, the programmer would have no idea where `cars` and `trucks` are located (and would not need to know).

The value of a variable at any given moment is the quantity stored at the location represented by that variable. When the value changes, the old value is replaced by the new. *The old value is destroyed.*

Example: **Variable Names**

In Program 1.2, the quantities `cars`, `trucks`, and `total` are the names of variables.

Note that nowhere in the program is there any indication of *where* any variables are stored. Knowing their names is all that is needed.

Variables are the main actors in a *C* program. The basic idea of virtually every *C* program is to do something that changes the values of the variables that are important for the problem at hand. It is the final values of those variables that represent a solution to the problem.

1.4

DATA TYPES

All information in a computer is stored as some combination of `1`'s and `0`'s. A grouping of eight of these is called a *byte*. (The size of a compartment referred to in the preceding section is one byte.) As it happens, there is more than one way to interpret a given byte. For example, this combination:

```
0 1 0 0 0 0 0 1
```

is treated as the integer `65` using one coding method, but as the character `A` using another coding method. If the above combination were stored in a variable called `Grade`, representing a student's grade, we could easily be confused about its meaning. Is the grade high (an `A`), or low (a `65`)? Clearly, knowing the combination of `1s` and `0s` is not enough; we must also know how the combination should be interpreted. In *C*, the proper interpretation is given by the variable's *data type*. We can define a data type as a description to the computer indicating how a quantity stored at a particular location is to be interpreted. The programming mechanism for doing this is called a *variable declaration*.

Example: **Variable Declarations**

In Program 1.2, there are two lines, `[7]` and `[8]`, which constitute the variable declarations for the program:

```
int      cars, trucks;
float    total=0.0;              /* insurance cost */
```

The first tells the computer to set aside locations for the variables `cars` and `trucks`, and to treat each of these quantities as integers. The second performs a similar function for `total`, and assigns it the value 0.0.[2]

For our purposes, we will mainly deal with the three data types given below:

Keyword	Meaning	Sample Values
char	letters, digits, symbols	'B', '$', '7', ':'
float	real numbers	32.4, 0.007
int	integers	7, -22

Note that values of type `char` are individual characters surrounded by single quote marks. Thus the *digit* `'7'` is different from the *integer* `7`. The three types listed above are examples of *scalar* data types; they cannot be decomposed into simpler types. In Chapter 6, we will encounter data types that are combinations of these scalar types, and therefore can be decomposed.

Both integers and floating point numbers are each represented in the computer as a multibyte quantity whose value is determined by various rules of binary arithmetic.[3] A character, however, is represented by a single byte. In the case of characters, the computer industry has agreed on the meaning of 128 of the possible 256 combinations of `1s` and `0s`. This set of designations is called the *ASCII code*; it is given in Appendix D. We often use the term *text* to characterize data whose individual bytes are treated as ASCII characters. We will see that text plays an important role in computing.

1.5

OPERATORS

We are all familiar with the notion of an operator; the arithmetic operator + is an example. Perhaps we can't give a dictionary-style definition for it, but we know what it *does*. In *C*, almost all operators fall into two categories: binary and unary.

---

2   The name `float` comes from `float`ing point, which refers to a number with a decimal point.

3   One need not know these rules in order to program!

Binary Operators

A *binary operator* causes a simple, well-defined interaction between two quantities. For example, `*` is a binary operator that means *multiply;* a "well-defined interaction" such as `8 * 4` is the familiar process of multiplication. The data values `8` and `4`, which are the quantities involved in this interaction, are known generically as *operands.* The interaction is more properly called the *operation.* The general form for a binary operation can be symbolized as:

$$\{<operand> <operator> <operand>\}$$

The " `< >`" notation is the way we will denote the general format of a program element. When writing a program, the angle brackets, along with what is between them, are to be replaced with specific instances of the indicated quantity. Thus, for example,

$$\{<operand> <operator> <operand>\}$$

might be replaced with "x + y".

In the absence of a dictionary-style definition, we will define binary operation by simply listing all possible "simple, well-defined interactions."[4] In the chart below, we have listed some of the binary operations that are familiar from arithmetic. There are many others, and they will be introduced as needed.

Symbol	Operation
	Addition
–	Subtraction
*	Multiplication
/	Division
%	Modulus

The last operation gives the remainder of integer division. This is the kind of division we learned in grade school; for example, `7 % 4` gives a quotient of `1` and a remainder of `3`.

Example: Binary Operations

In Program 1.2, we have the following instances of binary operations:

1. `CAR_RATE` and `cars` are multiplied, line `[11]`.
2. `TRUCK_RATE` and `trucks` are multiplied, line `[11]`.

---

4   This is a perfectly reasonable approach. How, for example, would we define `weekday`? By listing all possible weekdays. Of course, what makes it reasonable is that fact that we can easily list all possible weekdays. If there were ten thousand weekdays, we would have quite a problem!

3. The above two quantities are added, line [11].

4. CREDIT and total are added, line [12].

Unary Operators

A *unary operator* causes a simple, well-defined action to be taken on a single oper-
and. Following the strategy above, we define "simple, well defined action" by making a list. For now, we only need to know one unary operator[5]: the negation operator -.
This takes the value of an integer or floating point number and changes its sign.

Example: Unary Operation

In Program 1.2, the value 25 in the definition of CREDIT, line [4], is negated.

The general form of a unary operation is:

$$\{<\text{operator}> <\text{operand}>\}$$

Other unary operators will be introduced later as needed.

There are three extremely important questions regarding all operators that need
to be addressed:

- What are the possible data types of the operands?
- What is the data type of the result of the operation?
- If we have a combination of operators, which operation goes first?

The first issue is important because a given operation is not necessarily valid for all
types of operands. For example, it makes no sense to multiply two variables of type
char. Let us summarize what we are allowed to do with our present set of operators:

- We can add, subtract, multiply, and divide any pair of integers. The result is an
integer. We may also use the modulus operator on two integers. Thus the integer division problem 3 ÷ 5 has an integer quotient (3/5) of zero, and an integer remainder
(3%5) of 3.
- We can add, subtract, multiply, and divide any pair of floating point numbers.
The result is a floating point number. We may *not* use the modulus operator on two
floating point numbers. Note that the operations 3./5., 3./5, and 3/5. have an answer of 0.6, quite different from the integer operation noted above.
- We can add, subtract, multiply, and divide when one number is floating point
and the other is an integer. The result is a floating point number. We may *not* use the
modulus operator in this case.

---

5   We can also use + as a unary operator, by putting it in front of a number.

• In this text, we will avoid any of the above operations when the data are of type **char**.[6]

Precedence and Associativity

The third issue raised above—order of operations—is most critical. The issue arises when we have a sequence involving more than one operation.

Example: **Multiple Operations**

Consider line [11] from Program 1.2:

```
total = CAR_RATE * cars  +  TRUCK_RATE * trucks
```

Here we clearly have more than one operation.[7] Although the operators on the right are in the order *, +, * (whether we read from left to right, or right to left), the rules of algebra tell us that the addition operation is performed after the two multiplications have been done. Thus neither a left to right rule nor a right to left rule seems to be in effect.

We describe the above situation by saying that the * operator has a higher *precedence* than the + operator. That is, no matter where * appears in a sequence of + and * operations, the * operation is performed first. The table below lists *precedence rules* for arithmetic operations. In a sequence of operations, the one whose operator is highest in the table comes first.

Operator	**Precedence**
( )	Highest; quantities in parentheses are evaluated first; nested parentheses are evaluated innermost first
*, /, %	Second highest
+, –	Lowest

Example: **Operator Precedence**

Suppose that under some circumstances, our car dealer pays the car rate for both types of vehicles. Then we would change line [11] of Program 1.2 to this:

```
total = CAR_RATE * (cars + trucks)
```

Since the parentheses have the highest precedence, the operation in the parentheses is done first. The multiplication is done second.

---

6 It is possible, however, to do an operation such as 'a' + 1   to get 'b', but we will have no need for that capability.

7 The equal sign is also an operator. More on that in the next chapter.

Nothing that we have discussed above addresses the issue of what happens if a sequence of operations has *equal* precedence. In that case, the issue becomes one of *associativity*: do the operations proceed left to right, or right to left? Fortunately, almost all operators associate the same way: left to right. In Appendix E we have listed all the operators that we eventually use in this text and put them in precedence order. Those that associate from right to left are noted.

Examples: **Precedence and Associativity**

(a) $10 + (2 + 1) \% 4$
    Parentheses first: $(2 + 1) = 3; \rightarrow 10 + 3 \% 4$
    Modulus operator second: $3 \% 4 = 3 \rightarrow 10 + 3$
    Addition operator third: $10 + 3 = 13$

(b) $10 + 2 + 1 \% 4$
    Modulus operator first: $1 \% 4 = 1; \rightarrow 10 + 2 + 1$
    Equal precedence, do left to right: $10 + 2 = 12; 12 + 1 = 13$

(c) $3 * 4 / 2 \% 5$
    Equal precedence, do left to right: $3 * 4 = 12; 12 / 2 = 6; 6 \% 5 = 1$

(d) $8.0 / 4.0 * 2.0$
    Equal precedence, do left to right: $8.0 / 4.0 = 2.0; 2.0 * 2.0 = 4.0$

1.6

EXPRESSIONS

For now, we will define an *expression* as any legal combination of operands and operators. Of course, the only operators we have seen so far are arithmetic operators, so we are really talking about combinations of variables, constants, and operators that represent calculations. (We'll broaden our definition later.) The combination can have all or some of the above elements, i.e.:

1. A lone constant or variable.
2. Constant(s) and operator(s) only.
3. Variable(s) and operator(s) only.
4. Constant(s), variables(s), and operator(s).

Given the above possibilities, we can see that many things can qualify as expressions. That is certainly true for Program 1.2:

Examples: **A Variety of Expressions**

1. The values `30` and `7` of lines `[9]` and `[10]`.
2. The `-25` of line `[4]`.
3. The sum `total + credit` of line `[12]`.
4. The sum `CAR_RATE * cars + TRUCK_RATE * trucks`, line `[11]`.

Of course, for the last three categories, the combination must obey the rules of the operations involved. It would be incorrect, for example, if the expression in line [12] of Program 1.2 looked like this:

```
total   CREDIT   +
```

This does *not* match the general form of either a binary operation or a unary operation.

1.7

STATEMENTS

Technically, a *statement* is an expression that is terminated by a semicolon. Obviously, many things can thus qualify as statements, including statements that do nothing. For our purposes, it is useful to think of a statement as a program element that causes the computer to execute one of the five major actions described below. (We will study these statements in detail in the next two chapters.)

1. Input: Enables a program to accept information that is outside the computer's memory and store it in the memory. Program 1.2 does not have an input statement.

2. Output: Enables a program to deliver information to a place that is outside the computer's memory.

Example: **An Output Statement**
Line [12] of Program 1.2—`printf("%f", total + CREDIT);`—causes the result of the calculation to appear on the screen.

3. Assignment: Enables a program to store a value at a specified location.

Example: **Assignment Statements**
In Program 1.2, there are three places where assignments occur:

30 is stored at `cars` (line [9])

7 is stored at `trucks` (line [10])

`CAR_RATE * cars + TRUCK_RATE * trucks` is stored at `total` (line [11]).

4. Selection: Enables a program to follow different paths under different circumstances. For example, the player of a pinball machine simulator might have a choice of playing the game with the noises, or without. If the choice is *with noise*, a certain block of code is executed. If the choice is *no noise*, then a different block of code is executed. Program 1.2 does not have a selection statement.

5. Repetition: Enables a program to execute the same section of code over and over. This is one of the most important things a computer does, since many real world problems require that something be done repeatedly. For example, a computer can control a machine designed to produce eyeglass lenses. The lens is ground a certain amount, after which a measurement is taken. If the measurement is not within a specified tolerance, the grinding is repeated, and another measurement is taken. The entire process is repeated until the lens is within tolerance. The block of code that controls the grinding step is repeated as many times as needed. The block of code that controls the measurement step is also repeated. Program 1.2 does not have a repetition statement.

Normally, statements are executed in the order they are written in a program. Both selection and repetition statements allow for the possibility that the usual order may be overridden.

1.8

PROGRAM EXECUTION

We can now upgrade our definition of *program* slightly: It is a sequence of declarations, followed by a sequence of statements that a computer can execute. To write a good program, one needs to do serious thinking about how to solve the problem. Carrying out the result of that thinking, however, is rather mechanical. Basically, there are three steps:

1. Editing.
2. Compiling/preprocessing.
3. Linking/loading.

Editing means typing out the actual code, known as *source code*. This is done with a *text editor*, a program that enables a programmer to create, modify, save, and retrieve text. It is assumed that the reader is familiar with an editor.

Compiling means translating the source code, which is not readable by a computer, into *machine code*, which is. A program called a *compiler* does this, using the C source code as input. The output of a compiler is called *object code*.

The compiler does more than just translate. It checks whether or not the rules for constructing a C program have been obeyed. The collection of these rules is called the language's *syntax*. A violation of any of the rules is called a *syntax error*. When syntax errors exist in a program, the compiler outputs a list of those errors, but produces no object code. It is the programmer's job to correct those errors, then recompile the program. Experiment 1-1 deals in part with syntax errors.

Before the actual translation takes place, the source code undergoes various manipulations by a part of the C compiler called the *preprocessor*. One of these manipulations is the replacement of source code by other source code. Program 1.2 has three instances of this. The preprocessor replaces every occurrence of the identifier

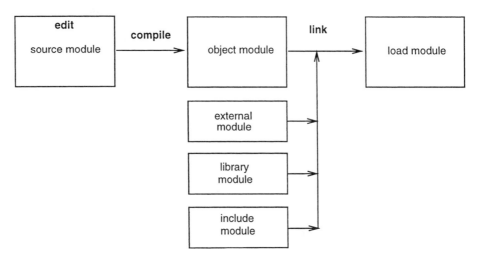

Figure 1.3   Compile, edit, and link stages.

CAR_RATE with the numerical value 20.5. It does the same thing for TRUCK_RATE and CREDIT.

Another preprocessor task is to include certain code that is external to the program, but vital for its execution. Program 1.2 has one instance of this in line [1]. Here, the preprocessor is asked to include a block of code called stdio.h. This code contains definitions of quantities needed for proper input and output performance.[8] stdio.h is an example of an external block of code called a *header file*. In *C* there are header files for different specialized purposes. For example, a header file called math.h is required when one wishes to do trigonometric calculations. In this text, we will only rarely need a header file other than stdio.h. We will note that need when the occasion arises.

As we can see from our program examples, the symbol # indicates that the line in the program is an instruction for the preprocessor.

Linking is the piecing together of different blocks object code into a single executable package called a *load module*. Where do these different blocks come from? In some cases, a very large program is compiled in separate sections; the different parts must eventually be tied together. Also, some of the functionality of *C* is provided by groups of precompiled routines called *libraries*. These need to be included in the final object code.

Loading is the placement of the object module in an appropriate place in the computer's memory. Once that is done, the computer can actually execute the program.

---

8   Program 1.1 ran without stdio.h, but in general it is not a good idea to leave it out. All our programs will include it.

The stages described above are shown schematically in Figure 1.3. The actual implementation of these steps depends on the computer system being used. Thus, we can describe the overall process only with the generalizations given above.

EXPERIMENT 1-1

(a) Type Program 1.2 above program into the computer, *without the line numbers, but otherwise exactly as it appears*, then compile it. It is important not to make any mistakes. (In a subsequent step, we will be instructed to make mistakes!)[9]

(b) Compile the same program again, but leave off one of the semicolons. The compiler will report a mistake. How closely did the compiler pinpoint the mistake?

(c) Repeat part (b) a few times, only make a different mistake each time. Get a feel for how the compiler deals with these problems.

(d) What does the compiler report when `car = 30;` replaces `cars = 30;`?

(e) Replace line [11] of the original program with the following:

```
total = CAR_RATE / 0;
```

Compile the program, then run it. What happened?

EXPERIMENT 1-2

We mentioned that the compiler ignores extra spaces, which allows us to indent program lines for readability. Suppose we didn't care about readability. What spaces could we leave out? Recompile the above program skeleton with these substitutions:

(a) `cars=30` instead of `cars = 30`.
(b) `intcars, trucks` instead of `int cars, trucks`.

Why is it that some spaces are necessary?

---

9 Depending on the compiler used, there may be a "warning." In general, a warning indicates something in a program that seems suspicious to the compiler. We can ignore any warnings in this program. Normally, though, a warning should be checked out. It may be something we should pay attention to, or it may be harmless.

Exercises

(1-1) Which of these are legal identifiers?

```
SHARK    3CPO    IF     .lion
Arbor    tail-or  3.14159    five
Part2    Part#2   SquareRoot   SqRt    Sq Rt
```

(1-2) Compute the value of each expression. Indicate the data type of the result.

```
a    12/5 + 3*3
b    6 + (25.2/1.5)/12
c    (14 % 5)/4
d    10 * 3/5
e    2*2;
f    2*2.0;
g    -5 % 2;
h    5 % -2;
i    -5 % -2;
```

(1-3) Translate each English phrase into a *C* expression. Use any variable name desired.

(a) Two times the weight of a car.

(b) The amount in a savings account after a hundred dollars is withdrawn.

(c) The amount in a savings account one year from now, assuming it is untouched, and draws simple interest.

(d) The character representing the dollar sign.

(1-4) Label these values as **char**, **int**, or neither.

```
43    2,348    B    Qu    ;    -13    0    0.0
```

(1-5) Which of these are valid symbolic constants?

```
6.6    char    3*Y    F    'F'
```

(1-6) Suppose a *C* program consists of two statements. Could they be written like this?

```
< statement 1 >
; < statement 2 > ;
```

(1-7) Find the syntax errors in this program:

```
main();
x int;
{ }
```

(1-8) Find the syntax errors in this program:

```
define x = 7;
  {
      main()
      int: z
  }
```

Programming Problems

(1-P1) Write a program that does all of the following:

(a) Tells the preprocessor to include the files **math.h** and **string.h**.

(b) Defines a floating point constant called PRESSURE whose value is 29.93.

(c) Declares an integer variable length that is initialized to 7.

(d) Declares a character variable letter.

Must this program be run in order to see if it is correct, or simply compiled?

PROGRAMS FOR CHAPTER ONE

Program 1.1: A One Liner

```
/* This program prints the message:

                Uh oh.  My first C program.

  on the screen. */

main()
  {
     printf("Uh oh.  My first C program");
  }
```

Program 1.2: A Sampler

```
/* This program calculates the cost of insuring a car dealer's
   stock against storm damage.  It includes crediting the
   dealer with overpayments from a previous bill. */

[1]   #include<stdio.h>
[2]   #define CAR_RATE      20.5    /* rate for insuring cars */
[3]   #define TRUCK_RATE    31      /* rate for insuring trucks */
[4]   #define CREDIT        -25     /* previous overcharge */
```

```
[5]     main()
[6]     {
[7]         int         cars, trucks;
[8]         float       total = 0.0;    /* insurance cost */

[9]         cars   =  30;          /* there are 30 cars */
[10]        trucks =  7;           /* there are  7 trucks */

        /* now add up rate times number of vehicles */

[11]        total = CAR_RATE * cars + TRUCK_RATE * trucks;

[12]      printf("%f", total + CREDIT);
[13]    }
```

2 Statements: Part I

Programs for Chapter Two

- Program 2.1: Output statements
- Program 2.2: Input statement

In the next two chapters, we will cover in detail the statements described very generally in the preceding chapter. Here, we concentrate on input and output, the mechanisms that enable a program to communicate with the outside world. We discuss output first so that we have a tool for examining the results of our experiments.

2.1

OUTPUT

For most of our purposes, *output* will mean characters written to the screen. Although modern screen output is often graphical, we will for the convenience of this discussion consider only the (somewhat) outdated text based screen, which typically displays 25 lines of output, each containing 80 characters. Hence, we can mentally divide the screen into 2000 cells, each capable of displaying one character. Every cell is associated with a one byte location in a special section of the memory reserved for video output. When the ASCII code for a character is stored in one of those locations, the corresponding character appears on the screen. This is illustrated schematically in Figure 2.1. Characters are written to the screen in the same order that they are written on this page: starting at the upper left, and ending at the lower right. The computer

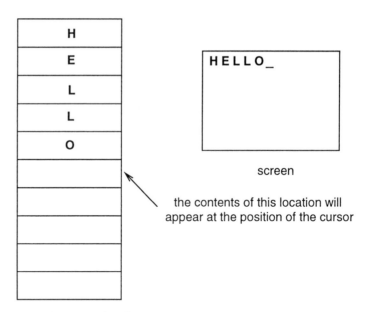

Figure 2.1   Schematic representation of screen output.

has an internal mechanism for keeping track of the location of the next character to be written. We see this as a unique mark on the screen called a *cursor*.

For output, we will use `printf`.[1] To illustrate this, we have modified Program 1.2 so that it contains several different `printf` statements. Program 2.1 shows the modified version. Each `printf` follows this general form:

```
printf("<control string>", <optional arguments>);
```

Essentially, the part called *control string* is what gets written to the screen. This is quite an oversimplification, though; to fill in the details, we need to look at a number of examples.

Example: Printing a Message

Line [1] of Program 2.1 illustrates how `printf` is used to output a message:

```
printf("The cost of the insurance is ...  ");
```

The control string in this case consists of the message we want to print. Everything between the quote marks—`The cost of insurance is ...`—is reproduced literally on the screen.

---

1 Technically, `printf` is a *function*, a programming construct that will be covered in Chapter 4. For now, it is fine to think of `printf` as our output statement (since we will always terminate it with a semicolon).

Note that in this case, there is *only* a control string; the part called *optional arguments* is absent. Another important fact about this `printf`: after it executes, the cursor is positioned just to the right of the last character printed.

Example: **Printing a Single Value**

Line [2] of Program 2.1 illustrates how `printf` is used to output a single value:

```
printf("%f", total + CREDIT);
```

Unlike the previous `printf`, this one has an argument: the quantity whose value we want to output. The control string in this case consists of a symbol called a *format specifier*. Each of the three data types we introduced in the previous chapter has its own format specifier as indicated in the table below. Note that the calculation `total + CREDIT` is done within the `printf` statement. When the actual output takes place, the numerical value of `total + CREDIT` replaces the format specifier.

In effect, this value of `total + CREDIT` ends up between the quote marks, and is therefore the value that is output. Since the previous `printf` left the cursor just to the right of the end of the previous message, this value is output immediately following the message. This `printf` also leaves the cursor just to the right of the last character output.

Data Type	Format Specifier
int	%d
float	%f
char	%c

Example: **Printing a Message and the Value of a Variable**

Line [3] of Program 2.1 illustrates how a single value can be output as part of a message:

```
printf(" \n Insurance costs %f dollars", total + CREDIT);
```

We have simply inserted the format specifier at the desired place in the message. The format specifier is replaced with the value of the variable. The modified control string is written to the screen.

This line contains the symbol `\n`. When it is encountered in a `printf` statement, the cursor jumps to the beginning of the next line. We want that to happen here, since we want the new output to occur on a new line. To accomplish the same task, we could have written the previous `printf` this way:

```
printf("%f \n", total + CREDIT);
```

Then the cursor would have been forced to the beginning of the next line immediately after the previous output.

The \n is an example of an *escape sequence*, a special code that causes the computer to do something out of the ordinary, as opposed to printing an actual character. In this text, the \n is the only escape sequence we will need.

Example: **Printing the Values of More than One Variable**

Line [4] of Program 2.1 illustrates how two values can be output in a single printf statement:

```
printf("\n %d vehicles cost %f dollars", cars+trucks, total+credit);
```

Here we want to print a message stating the cost of insuring only the cars, along with how many cars we have. We put a format specifier in the control string at each place where we want a numerical value to appear. We also list the values to be output in the *optional arguments* section in exactly the same order as their corresponding format specifiers appear in the control string.

EXPERIMENT 2-1

(a) Write a program that prints the value of a real number, but mistakenly uses the %d format specifier. What happens? Does the compiler flag the error?

(b) Repeat the above, but try to print integers using noninteger format specifiers. Note the results.

(c) Now print the character 'A' using the integer format specifier. What is the significance of the numerical value output?

(d) We noted that it is possible to add an integer to a character. Try printing the quantity 'A' + 7, first with %c, then with %d. What happens?

(e) When printing two values, say, integers, must there be a space between the format specifiers? Can there be more than one space?

EXPERIMENT 2-2

In Chapter 1, we discussed the idea of operator precedence. In this experiment, we present a scheme for determining precedence rules by investigating pairs of expressions that look like this:

```
a <operator1> b <operator2> c
a <operator2> b <operator1> c
```

where a, b, and c are the operands. The idea is to see if the two operations are done, say, from left to right in both cases, or if one of the operations is always done first, no matter where it is. If the latter is true, then the operation that is done first has higher precedence. If the former is true, both operations have equal precedence.

(a) Run a program that outputs the expressions (8 + 4 * 2) and (8 * 4 + 2). This will confirm what we know about multiplication versus addition, namely, that these operations are *not* done left to right in both cases.

(b) Repeat the above experiment to test the following pairs:

  1. / and *

  2. % and -

  3. / and +

EXPERIMENT 2-3

(a) Declare two integers, x and y. Make the assignments x = 3 and y = 5. Then run a program with these printf statements:

```
printf("%1d %1d \n", x,y);
printf("%2d %2d \n", x,y);
printf("%10d %10d \n", x,y);
```

What is the effect of the numbers immediately following the % symbol?

(b) Now declare a real variable, a, and assign -368.555 to it. Run a program with these printf statements:

```
printf("%f \n", a);
printf("%10.2f \n", a);
```

What does the number preceding the point do? Is its effect any different from that seen in the int case? What does the number following the point do?

(c) What does the computer do in this case: printf("%2f \n", a)?

Exercises

(2-1) Consider this pair of printf statements:

```
printf("%d %d %d \n", x,y,z);
printf("%d %d %d \n", z,x,y);
```

Which set of outputs makes sense?

500	700	900
500	900	700
900	700	500
500	700	900
700	500	900
500	900	700
500	700	900
900	500	700

(2-2) Give the output of this code exactly as it appears on the screen.

```
printf("The quick brown \n");
printf("fox jumped");
printf("over the lazy \n");
printf("dog.");
```

(2-3) `Tracing` a program means going through it step by step, keeping track of the value of each variable at each step. Trace the following program:

```
#define c 25
main()
{ int x, y, z;
  x = 8;
  z = x*c;
  y = z - x;
  x = x + z;
  printf("%d %d %d \n", x,z,y);
}
```

2.2

ASSIGNMENT

In an *assignment* statement, the value of a variable is replaced with the value of an expression.

Example: Assignment Statements

Program 2.1 has three assignment statements:

```
cars   =  30;
trucks =  7;
total = CAR_RATE * cars + TRUCK_RATE * trucks;
```

In the first two, explicit values are assigned to the variable. In the third, a value is calculated first, then assigned to the variable.

The symbol " = " is called the *assignment operator*. It is a binary operator[2] whose operands follow this general form:

```
<variable> = <expression>
```

The order above is important. One cannot, for example, make the assignment the other way. Note that the above is itself an expression, since it is a legal combination of operands and operators. When a semicolon is placed immediately following:

---

2 With a lower precedence than the arithmetic operators.

```
<variable> = <expression>;   <--- note semicolon!
```

it becomes an assignment *statement*.

Since an assignment statement *looks* like an equation, we might think that it *be-haves* like an equation. For example, in an algebra class, we would interpret the equation

$$z = x + y$$

as "add **x** and **y**, and call the result **z**." In *C*, we interpret it this way:

Examine the contents of locations **x** and **y**. Take their sum, then replace the contents of location **z** with this sum.

The reason for thinking in terms of *contents of locations* should be apparent from the following example:

$$z = z + x$$

We could never get away with this in algebra, but in *C* it makes perfect sense:

Examine the contents of **z** and **x**. Take their sum and replace the existing contents of location **z** with this sum.

Figure 2.2 illustrates the above idea schematically. Note that the contents of location **x** do not change.

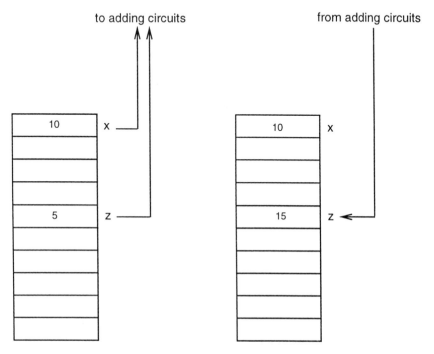

Figure 2.2   How the statement "z = z + x" is executed. (a) Copies of **x** and **z** are sent to an adding circuit outside the memory. (b) Adding circuit returns the result, which is written to **z**.

The issue of data types in an assignment statement is very important. Suppose, for example, that z is declared as `float`, while x is declared as `int`. Then anything we wish to store in z must be in the form of a floating point number. Mathematically, a floating point number is simply a real number. Certainly, all integers are real numbers, so we should be able to assign them to z. That is, we should be able to write something like this:

```
z = x;
```

and not get into any trouble. The computer, however, internally represents an integer differently from a floating point number. Thus the x as it stands cannot be stored in location z. Its internal representation must first be changed to that of a floating point number of equivalent value. (For example, a 3 must be changed to a 3.0.) Then the x can be stored in z. The C compiler makes this change automatically when the above assignment of x is made. Note that this change is only a temporary expedient for the current problem; values stored at x are still treated as integers.

The data type conversion process described above is called *promotion*. If promotion did not exist, we would need to make sure that both sides of an assignment statement are *exactly* the same data type. Instead, we can be a bit lax; we can assign an integer to a floating point number and get away with it. Unfortunately, the C compiler promotes under a variety of circumstances, not all of which are beneficial. This will be apparent from the next experiment. Therefore, except when assigning `int` to `float`, we should make sure that both sides of an assignment statement are exactly the same data type.

EXPERIMENT 2-4

See what the compiler does when a variable of type `float` is assigned to a variable of type `int`. Does such an assignment make sense logically? Experiment with all the possibilities of `int`, `float`, and `char` assigned to each other. Make sure to print out all the results of the assignments!

Summary of Programs 1.2 and 2.1:

Strategy: In both of these examples, assignment statements are used to assign values to the variables `cars` and `trucks`. The program takes a product of each of these variables with a number representing a rate, adds the two products, and assigns the result to the variable `total`. Finally, the total cost of insurance, reflecting the amount credited, is printed using one or more variants of `printf`.

Style:
- Comments are used to indicate the meaning of each constant and variable.
- All lines of `main` are uniformly indented.

- Meaningful, yet reasonably short, identifiers are used.
- Declarations are separated from the remaining statements in `main`.
- Binary operators have spaces on either side to enhance readability.
- Unary operators are connected without any space to their operand (for example, `-25`).
- Only one program statement is used per line.

Exercises

(2-4) Indicate whether these assignment statements are legal or illegal. Assume a, b, and x are integers; anything else is real.

```
(a)     x = FLOAT;
(b)     x = define;
(c)     x = x + x;
(d)     x = x*x;
(e)     x = #x;
(f)     x = a % b;
(g)     x = 10;
(h)     x = x/x;
(i)     x = a = b;
(j)     PerCent = 15%;
(k)     a = ((b)) + c;
```

(2-5) A pair of assignment statements can sometimes be written as single assignments. For example, consider the pair

```
x = y + z % 3;
x = y - 10;
```

The first of the two lines is irrelevant. Regardless of how **x** is changed by it, **x** will be changed again by the next statement. Therefore, the pair could be replaced by a single statement, namely, the second statement. Write the next two pairs as single assignments.

```
(a)     x = x + 6;
        x = 5*x - 5;
(b)     x = z*x;
        x = x % z;
```

(2-6) Suppose we have two variables, x and y. What code do we need in order to exchange their contents?

2.3

INPUT

For now, we will assume that input to our programs comes from the keyboard. When a key is pressed, a unique code is generated electronically. This code goes into a reserved area of the computer's memory known as the *keyboard buffer*. (In general, a buffer is an area of the computer's memory set aside as a temporary workspace for dealing with data.) Figure 2.3 illustrates a hypothetical keyboard buffer containing ten keystrokes, including spaces. When the program calls for keyboard input, it looks in the keyboard buffer, not at the keyboard itself, for the input. We say the program *reads* from the buffer. If the buffer is empty, the program pauses until the user types in the required input, then presses the ENTER key or its equivalent. The computer has an internal mechanism for keeping track of the next character to be read. Unlike the cursor, which marks the next position for output, this mechanism is not visible to us. When trying to understand the input process, then, we will have to keep track of this on our own. For example, at this point, the 3 is the next keystroke to be read in Figure 2.3.

The name of the input statement that we will use throughout this book is **scanf**.[3] It has this general format:

```
scanf("<format specifiers>", <variable addresses>);
```

Essentially, the *format specifiers* part indicate the type of data to be input, while the *variable addresses* part denotes the places where data are to be stored.

Examples: Input

```
(1) scanf("%f", &real_variable);   <- read a floating point number.
(2) scanf("%c", &char_variable);   <- read a character.
```

Note the **&** preceding the variable name. In this context, the **&** is a unary operator that means "address of." When this symbol is placed in front of a variable name, the resulting expression evaluates to the address of that variable. Hence, **scanf** stores the input value at the address of the variable. Once again we point out that the numerical value of the address is of no concern to us. The reference to the address is sufficient.

Figure 2.3   Hypothetical keyboard buffer.

---

3 This, like **printf**, is a function.

Example: **Input of Two Values**

In Program 2.2, the number of cars and trucks is input from the keyboard, rather than coded into the program. Lines [9] and [10] of Program 1.2 have been replaced by line [2] of Program 2.2:

```
scanf("%d %d", &cars, &trucks);
```

This statement tells the computer to look in the keyboard buffer for two integers. The value of the first integer is stored in the location reserved for `cars`, while the value of the second integer is stored in the location reserved for `trucks`.

It is the responsibility of the programmer to match the *k-th* entry in the *variable locations* part with the *k-th* format specifier. It is the responsibility of the user typing at the keyboard to enter the values in the correct order.

A Closer Look at `scanf` in Action

Let us assume that the user has typed the input shown in Figure 2.3 in response to this statement:

```
scanf("%f", &r);
```

Here, it is assumed that `r` has been previously declared as type `float`. Note that two numbers have been typed into the buffer, not one. After ENTER is pressed, the process of reading from the buffer begins. Starting from the beginning of the buffer, but skipping blanks, the computer examines each keystroke. It looks for the first occurrence of a character that can legitimately begin a floating point number. Then it treats each subsequent character as part of the number until it encounters a character that doesn't belong. In Figure 2.3, the 3 is the first legitimate character. Looking at the characters that follow consecutively, we see that the space immediately following the second 6 doesn't belong. Therefore, the three intervening characters—the decimal point and the two 6's—are treated as part of the number. Having read these four *characters*, the computer converts them to the *number* 3.66 and assigns this value to r. Since only one variable is called for in the `scanf` function, and one value has been obtained, the computer looks no further in the keyboard buffer. Note that the next `scanf` would begin at the character following the second 6.

Now let's see what happens when `scanf` requires two inputs. Consider this statement:

```
scanf("%f %d", &r, &n);
```

Here, the computer is instructed to look in the keyboard buffer for a floating point number, followed by an integer. Again we will assume that the numbers in Figure 2.3 comprise the input. As in the previous example, the computer examines each character starting from the beginning of the buffer. The process of reading the 3.66, and storing it in &r, is the same as before, so we can pick up the action from there. Recall that the next character to be read is the blank immediately following the second 6.

Since two variables are listed in the `scanf` statement, the computer does not stop after reading the `3.66`, but continues to read from the buffer. It ignores the spaces following the `3.66`, and treats the `5` as the start of an integer. The next two characters are legitimate ones for an integer, so they are read. Only when the computer encounters the space following the `8` does it cease reading. The three characters `5`, `2`, and `8` are converted to the integer `528`, and this value is stored at the address of `n`. A subsequent `scanf` would begin reading at the space following the `8`. Since values for both variables have now been read in, the `scanf` statement is finished, and the program moves on to the next statement.

The action of the `scanf` statement is really quite remarkable. It takes text input from the keyboard—individual ASCII characters—and automatically converts sequences of these characters to precisely the data type specified by the programmer in the control string.

EXPERIMENT 2-5

Write a program with these input and output statements:

```
scanf("%d", &a);
printf("%d \n", a);
scanf("%d", &b);
printf("%d \n", b);
```

Enter these numbers: 63 54 as one line of input. Did the computer stop at the second `scanf` statement? Explain why.

So far, the examples have been chosen so that the computer discovers the end of a number by encountering a space. In the next experiment, we consider what happens when something other than a space marks the end.

EXPERIMENT 2-6

Write a program with a `scanf` statement that inputs a single integer. Include a statement that prints the input value to the screen. Enter the value `537J` as the input. What happens?

The next experiment mixes character and numeric input.

EXPERIMENT 2-7

Write a program with this `scanf` statement:

```
scanf("%d %c", &i, &ch);
```

(a) Have the program print out the values that are input. Run the program three times, each with a different input: `8J` (no spaces between the two); `8 J` (one space); `8    J` (more than one space). Explain the results.

(b) Now use this `scanf`:

```
scanf("%c %d", &ch, &i);
```

and input the following: J8 (no spaces); J8 (one space before the J); J8 (at least two spaces before the J). Explain.

(c) Use the same `scanf` as (b), but input 8J without any spaces, then with at least one space before the 8. Explain.

Input should always be *prompted*, that is, preceded by a message telling the user something about what should be typed in.

Example: An Input Prompt

In Program 2.2, line [1] is a prompt for the `scanf` statement that follows it. Note that the cursor is left a few spaces to the right of the last character printed, so that the input is on the same line as the prompt.

```
printf("Enter the number of cars, then the number of trucks:    ");
scanf("%d  %d", &cars, &trucks);
```

Summary of Program 2.2:

Strategy: This program is virtually identical to Program 2.1. Instead of initializing the values of `cars` and `trucks` in the declarations, however, these values are read in using `scanf`. From that point on, the calculation is the same as in Program 2.1.

Style: The input statement is preceded by a prompt so that the user of the program knows what values to input.

Exercises

(2-7) Trace the following program given this input:

```
                3    7
                1    4

    main()
    { int x, y, z;
      scanf("%d %d %d", &x, &y, &z);
      x = y % z;
      z = y - x;
      y = y/z;
      x = x + z;
      printf("%d %d %d \n", x, y, z);
    }
```

Programming Problems

(2-P1) Write a program that does nothing.

(2P-2) Write a program that prints a blank line.

> *User Input:* Nothing.

> *Program Output:* A blank line (cursor drops to the beginning of the next line).

(2P-3) Write a program that prints a picture of a triangle.

> *User Input:* Nothing.

> *Program Output:* A triangle composed of asterisks.

(2P-4) Write a program that prints an American-style date given a European-style date.

> *User Input:* A date written as DD-MM-YY (day-month-year)

> *Program Output:* A date written as MM-DD-YY.

(2P-5) Write a program that computes the total price of a commodity.

> *User Input:* Price, followed by sales tax rate in percent.

> *Program Output:* The statement `The total price is XX`, with `XX` replaced by the total price.

(2-P6) Write a program with no assignment statements that prints the product of a real number and an integer.

> *User Input:* A real number, followed by an integer.

> *Program Output:* The statement `The product is XX`. with `XX` replaced by the actual product.

(2P-7) Write a program that converts a temperature measurement expressed in Celsius to one expressed in Fahrenheit.

> *User Input:* A floating point number representing Celsius temperature.

> *Program Output:* A prompt for the input. Also, the statement `The Fahrenheit equivalent of XXX is YYY`, with `XXX` replaced by the Celsius value, and `YYY` replaced by the Fahrenheit value.

(**2-P8**) Write a program that allows a user to choose an item from a menu.

User Input: An integer representing a menu selection, entered on the line indicated in the `Program Output` description, below.

Program Output: (a) A screen that (literally) has the following:

Choose one of the following :

1. < choice one >
2. < choice two >
3. < choice three >
4. < choice four >

Enter your choice here ... .

(b) The statement `Your choice is XXX`, with `XXX` replaced by the menu number. This statement must appear three lines below the menu.

PROGRAMS FOR CHAPTER TWO

Program 2.1: Output Statements

```
#include<stdio.h>
#define CAR_RATE      20.5
#define TRUCK_RATE    31
#define CREDIT        -25

main()
  {
  int          cars, trucks;
  float        total;
  cars   =  30;       /* there are 30 cars */
  trucks =  7;        /* there are  7 trucks */
  total = CAR_RATE * cars + TRUCK_RATE * trucks;

       /*  One way to output the information. */

[1]   printf("The cost of the insurance is ...   ");
[2]   printf("%f", total + CREDIT);

       /*  Another way to do it. */

[3]   printf(" \n Insurance costs %f dollars", total + CREDIT);

       /*  Yet another way. */
```

```
[4]    printf("\n %d vehicles cost %f dollars", cars+trucks,
                total+CREDIT);
       }
```

Program 2.2: Input Statement

```
#include<stdio.h>
#define CAR_RATE      20.5
#define TRUCK_RATE    31
#define CREDIT        -25

main()
  {
  int          cars, trucks;
  float        total;

      /* Tell the user how to input the information */

[1]   printf("Enter the number of cars, then the number of
            trucks:   ");
[2]   scanf("%d %d", &cars, &trucks);    /* input statement */

    total = CAR_RATE * cars + TRUCK_RATE * trucks;
    printf("The insurance cost is %f dollars", total + CREDIT);
    }
```

3 Statements: Part II

Programs for Chapter Three

- Program 3.1: Selection using an **if** statement
- Program 3.2: Selection using an **if-else** statement
- Program 3.3: Selection using a **switch** statement
- Program 3.4: Repetition using a **for** statement
- Program 3.5: Repetition using a **while** statement

We continue our discussion of the basic *C* statements with three selection statements and two repetition statements. Recall that, with these statements, decisions are made that allow for changes in the order in which statements execute.

Both selection and repetition statements depend on expressions involving operators we have not yet discussed. These are the so-called *relational operators*, which are used to compare the sizes of quantities. The table below lists each relational operator, its use in an expression (a *relational expression*), and how the expression is interpreted:

Operator	Example	Interpretation
<	a < b	Is **a** less than **b**?
>	a > b	Is **a** greater than **b**?
==	a == b	Is **a** equal to **b**?
!=	a != b	Is **a** different from **b**?
<=	a <= b	Is **a** less than or equal to **b**?
>=	a >= b	Is **a** greater than or equal to **b**?

If the answer to a question in the right-hand column is *yes*, then the corresponding relational expression in the middle column is taken to be *true*. If the answer is *no*, the expression is taken to be *false*. The truth or falsity of a relational expression is used as the basis for decisions made by selection and repetition statements.

From Appendix E, we see that all these operators have lower precedence than the arithmetic operators, and higher precedence than the assignment operator.

3.1

SELECTION

A selection statement enables a program to choose one of (possibly) several alternative sections of code. The choice is made while the program is running, but the criterion for deciding the choice is set when the program is written.

In this section, we have modified our original sample program so that we can illustrate selection. We have assumed that business for our hypothetical used car dealer is starting to pick up; certain discounts in insurance rates kick in if more than *50* cars are involved.

3.1.1 The `if` Statement

The simplest selection statement, called an `if` statement, enables a program either to take a particular action, or not to take it. The `if` statement is illustrated schematically in Figure 3.1. If `E` is *true*, then `F` executes. Otherwise, `F` is skipped.

Example: **An `if` Statement**

Program 3-1 contains an `if` statement in line [1]:

```
if (cars > 50)
  {
  total = 0.9 * total;
  printf("You qualify for a discount of ten percent. \n");
  printf("The stock exceeds the minimum by %d. \n", cars - 50);
  }
```

In this example, the three statements between the braces are executed if the expression `cars > 50` is *true*. If `cars > 50` is *false*, the three statements are bypassed, and execution proceeds with line [2] of the program. Note that the three statements are treated as a single unit; either *all* of them are executed, or *none* of them is. Any group of statements that is treated as a single unit is called a *compound statement*. Typically, then, an `if` statement has this general form:

```
if (<condition>)
    {
      <compound statement>
    };
```

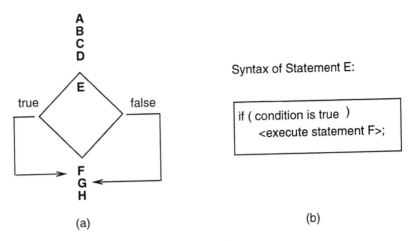

Syntax of Statement E:

```
if ( condition is true )
     <execute statement F>;
```

(a)   (b)

Figure 3.1   The `if` statement. (a) Schematic diagram. (b) Syntax.

Examples: Compound Statements

```
if (x <= 10)
   {
       x = x + 5;
       y = 2 * x;
   }

if (x != 10)
   {
       scanf("%d", &x);
       if (x < 2)
          x = x + 5;
   }

if (x != 10)
   {
       scanf("%d", &x);     <- OK to use braces anyway.
   }
```

For convenience, we will refer to the statements that get executed if the condition evaluates to *true* as the *body*. The `if( ... )` part will be called the *header*.

Internally, relational expressions have values that are numerical, not the *true* or *false* that we have been using for our discussions. In particular, an expression that is *false* evaluates to 0. Conversely, a relational expression that evaluates to 0 is considered *false*. If a relational expression is *true*, it evaluates to 1. However, a relational expression does not have to evaluate to 1 to be considered *true*. Those that evaluate to anything other than 0 are also considered true.

Examples: Relational Expressions

```
1. x = 5 < 10;      x evaluates to 0
2. x = x > x;       x ends up equal to 0
3. x = x >= x;      x ends up equal to 1
```

The next experiment will drive home the point that the condition in the `if` header is not quite as simple an issue as it seems.

EXPERIMENT 3-1

Suppose the condition part of the `if` contains a typing error: one = symbol instead of two:

```
if (temp = 100)
   printf("We are at the boiling point.");
```

Write a program that assigns a value of 50 to `temp`, then executes the `if` statement above. Did the `if` statement execute in a manner consistent with the fact that `temp` ≠ 100?

It is possible to *nest* the `if` statements, that is, embed one in another:

```
if (x > 5)
  if (y > 10)
    printf("Hello \n");
```

In the above example, *Hello* will not be printed unless both of the conditions are true.

Summary of Program 3.1

Strategy: This program is an extension of Program 2.2. The values of `cars` and `trucks` are read in using `scanf`, and the cost of insurance, `total`, is calculated exactly as before. Then an `if` statement is used to determine if the number of cars exceeds 50. If that is the case, `total` is replaced by 0.9 times its calculated value, and a message is printed out indicating that a discount has been applied. If the number of cars does not exceed 50, nothing happens to the calculated value of `total`, and no message is printed. Finally, the total cost of insurance, including the credited amount, is printed out.

Style: The body of the `if` statement is indented with respect to the header.

Exercises

One must be careful when dealing with consecutive `if` statements whose conditions involve the same variable. For example, consider this pair:

```
if (x >= 10)
     x = 6*x;
if (x >= 60)
     x = x/3;
```

If x starts out equal to or greater than 10, it will automatically be equal to or greater than 60 by the time the second if has been reached. Thus the second if statement is unnecessary; a single one will do the job:

```
if (x >= 10)
    x = 2*x;
```

For the three cases that follow, reduce the comparisons to a single if statement.

```
(3-1) if (x >= 10)
          x = x + 12;
      if (x >= 22)
          x = x % 22;
(3-2) if (x <= 10)
          x = x - 5;
      if (x <= 5)
          x = x - 5;
(3-3) if (x >= 10)
          x = 10 + x % 10;
      if (x > 20)
          x = x/2;
```

3.1.2 The if-else Statement

Line [2] of Program 3.1 printed a message to the dealer only if the stock was large enough to qualify for a discount on insurance rates. It might be more useful for the dealer if the program printed a message regardless of the size of the stock. Our program can do this with the if-else statement, an alternative form of the if that enables a program to choose one of two distinct alternatives, as opposed to doing something or not doing something. Figure 3.2 illustrates the if-else statement schematically.

Example: An if-else Statement

Line [1] of Program 3.2 illustrates the idea of branching to two different possibilities:

```
if (cars > 50)
  {
   total = 0.9 * total;
   printf("You qualify for a discount of ten percent. \n");
   printf("The stock exceeds the minimum by %d. \n", cars - 50);
  }
else
  {
   printf("You do not qualify for a discount. \n");
   printf("The stock is below minimum by %d. \n", 50 - cars);
  }
```

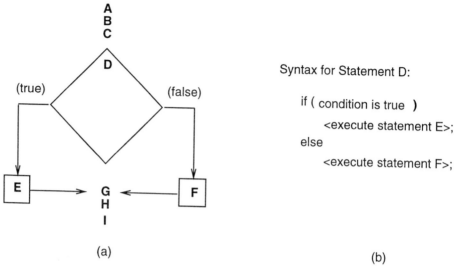

Syntax for Statement D:

if (condition is true)

        <execute statement E>;

else

        <execute statement F>;

        (a)   (b)

Figure 3.2 The `if-else` statement. (a) Schematic diagram. (b) Syntax.

If the expression `cars > 50` is *true*, the first compound statement executes. If the expression `cars > 50` is *false*, the second compound statement executes. In other words, regardless of the truth of the condition, *something* is done.

Typically, an `if-else` statement has this general form:

```
if (<condition>)
    {
       <compound statement>
    };
else
    {
       <compound statement>
    };
```

Examples: `if-else` **Statements:**

```
if (x > 5)
      printf("hello \n");
else if (x < 0)
         printf("goodbye \n");

if (x > 10)
    z = x + 8;
else;                  <- Legal.  Means don't do anything for the
                                  "else" part.

if (x > 10);                      <- Legal.  Means don't do anything
else printf("hello \n");                     for the "if" part.

if (0)                 <- Always false! "else" always done.
    x = x + 1;
```

```
else
    x = x - 1;

if (1)              <- Always true! "if" always done.
    x = x + 1;
else
    x = x - 1;
```

The second and third examples above illustrate the *empty statement*, a statement that does nothing. Occasionally, a statement that does nothing can be useful. Consider this situation:

```
if (x > 5)
    if (y > 10)
        printf("Hello \n");
else printf("Goodbye \n");
```

Clearly both conditions must be true in order for `Hello` to print. But what about `Goodbye`? Is the `else` part of the first `if` or the second? The indentation implies that it belongs to the first one. This situation calls for an experiment.

EXPERIMENT 3-2

   (a) Write a program with the above code. Assume that the `else` goes with the first `if`. In that case, setting `x` to an appropriate value such as **4** should cause `Goodbye` to print. Does this happen? What does the result say about where the `else` belongs?

   (b) If this is not convincing, continue to assume that the `else` belongs to the first `if`, but set both `x` and `y` to **6**. This makes the first `if` true; so based on our assumption, `Goodbye` shouldn't print. What actually happens? Explain.

From the above experiment, we can see that the `else` belongs to the second `if`, which is the closer of the two `if`'s. Suppose, however, we really want the `Goodbye` in the above example to go with the first `if`. We can accomplish this with the empty statement:

```
if (x > 5)
    if (y > 10)
        printf("Hello \n");
    else;
else printf("Goodbye \n");
```

The empty statement belongs with the inner `if-else`; the other `else` therefore belongs to the outer `if`. In general, an `else` goes with the nearest `if` providing the `if` meets two conditions:

1. It is the `if` part of an `if-else` statement.

2. It is not already paired with an `else`.

Logical Operators

Up to now, our selection statements have depended on very simple conditions: `cars > 50`, `temperature == 100`, etc. In the real world, actions can depend on two conditions simultaneously: *If she is arthritic* AND *is also taking blood pressure medication, then we recommend ten minutes a day of exercise.* This construct can be easily programmed, but it requires the use of another type of operator called a *logical operator*. We need to know about three such operators; the table that follows summarizes their behaviors. In the table, we have assumed that S_1 and S_2 are two relational expressions, so that each evaluates to *true* or *false*.

Symbol	Logical Operation	Use and Meaning
&&	AND	S_1 && S_2. This expression evaluates to *false* unless both S_1 and S_2 are *true*.
||	OR	S_1 || S_2. This expression evaluates to *true* unless both S_1 and S_2 are *false*.
!	NOT	!S_1. Evaluates to *false* if S_1 is *true*; evaluates to *true* if S_1 is *false*.

Examples: Logical Operators

```
if ( (x > 50) && (y > 50) )
    printf("Hallelujah! \n");

if ( !(x < 10) || (y == 10) )
    printf("Too bad.  \n");
```

We can make the `if` condition in Program 3.2 more stringent:

```
if ( (cars > 50) && (trucks > 25) )
  {
    total = 0.9 * total;
    printf("You qualify for a discount of ten percent. \n");
    printf("The stock exceeds the minimum. \n");
  }
else
  {
    printf("You do not qualify for a discount. \n");
    printf("The stock is below minimum. \n");
  }
```

In the above, `cars` must be greater than `50` and `trucks` must be greater than `25` in order for the first set of statements to execute. If either of those conditions does not hold, then the second set of statements will execute. Note that according to the precedence rules, the nested parentheses are unnecessary; they are there to emphasize visually the two individual conditions.

EXPERIMENT 3-3

(a) Suppose we have three integers—a, b, and c—and we want to see if a < b < c. Can the if statement be written like this?

```
if (a < b < c)
   printf("It sure is! \n");
```

Test the above with these values: a = 4, b = 5, and c = 6. Does this code behave in a manner consistent with the mathematical relationship between *a*, *b*, and c?

(b) Repeat the above, only test it using c > b > a. The result should be the same. Is it? Explain what happens. What's the best way to make a test like this?

Summary of Program 3.2

Strategy: This program reads in the values of cars and trucks as before, and calculates the value of total. An if-else statement determines if the number of cars exceeds 50. If it does, the value of total is reduced, and a message is printed out. If the number of cars does not exceed 50, then a different message is printed out; total is not reduced. Finally, the total cost of insurance is printed out, including the amount credited.

Style: The statements comprising the if and else parts of the if-else are uniformly indented with respect to the keywords if and else.

Exercises

In some unusual circumstances, an if statement can be written as an assignment statement. For example, this if-else statement

```
if (a < b)
    x = 1;
else x = 0;
```

can be written this way: x = a < b.[1] Rewrite each of the selection statements below as an assignment statement in which the variable p takes on the value of a relational expression.

(3-4)
```
if (x == 10)
   if (x == 5)
      p = 0;
```

---
1 x will be assigned either a 0 or 1, depending on the value of a < b.

```
              else p = 1;
          else p = 1;
```

(3-5)
```
          if (x == 10)
              if (y == 5)
                  p = 0;
              else p = 1;
          else p = 1;
```

(3-6)
```
          if ((x > 2) || (x < 2))
              p = 0;
          else p = 1;
```

(3-7)
```
          if ((x > 2)  || (x > 7))
              p = 0;
          else p = 1;
```

(3-8)
```
          if ((x > 2) && (y < 2))
              if (z == 5)
                  p = 1;
              else p = 0;
          else p = 0;
```

(3-9)
```
          if ((x > 2) && (y < 2))
              if (z == 5)
                  p = 1;
              else p = 0;
          else p = 1;
```

(3-10) Write this statement without any nesting.
```
          if ((x > 2))
              if (z == 5)
                  y = 7;
              else y = 12;
          else y = 12;
```

(3-11) Write this as two `if` statements (no `else`!).
```
          if (x < 17)
              y = 7;
          else y = 12;
```

3.1.3 The `switch` Statement

For our hypothetical used car dealer, business is getting a bit more complicated: the insurance company has developed a scheme using three different rate classes, num-

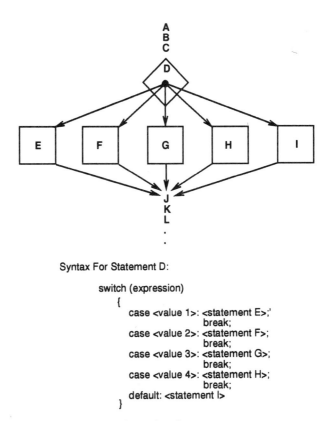

Syntax For Statement D:

```
switch (expression)
    {
        case <value 1>: <statement E>;'
                        break;
        case <value 2>: <statement F>;
                        break;
        case <value 3>: <statement G>;
                        break;
        case <value 4>: <statement H>;
                        break;
        default: <statement I>
    }
```

Figure 3.3 Schematic diagram of the usual operation of a `switch` statement.

bered 1, 2, and 3, which it uses to decide the cost of insurance. A program that takes account of this new twist must therefore be able to branch to a choice of at least three different directions. A combination of `if` statements (see Exercise 3-12) could accomplish this, but there is a much neater way using the so-called `switch` statement. The usual operation of the `switch` statement is illustrated in Figure 3.3. In this diagram, one of the five statements—E, F, G, H or I—executes depending on the value of the `switch` statement, D.

Example: **Multiway Branching Using** switch

Line [1] of Program 3.3 illustrates a three-way branch based on the value of the variable `rate_class`:

```
switch (rate_class) {
  case 1:
    cost = 22.3*(cars + bikes) + 26.1*trucks;
    printf("The cost for insurance is %f dollars \n", cost);
    break;
  case 2:
```

```
        cost = 24.5*(trucks + bikes) 22.3*cars;
        printf("The cost for insurance is %f dollars \n", cost);
        break;
      case 3:
        cost = 22.3*(bikes + trucks) + 24.5*cars;
        printf("The cost for insurance is %f dollars \n", cost);
        break;
      default: printf("You have entered an invalid rate class. \n");
      }
```

Depending on the value of `rate_class`, one of the sections above will execute. (A more detailed explanation follows below.)

Basically, a `switch` statement is composed of two parts:

1. A *header* consisting of the keyword `switch` followed by an expression enclosed in parentheses.

2. A *body* consisting of all possible choices, with each choice prefaced by the keyword `case`.

The `switch` statement works like this: If the expression in the header evaluates to one of the `cases` in the body, the statements associated with that `case` are executed. If the value of the expression is not on the list of cases, the statements associated with `default` are executed. In both cases, after the appropriate section has been executed, the program continues with the statement immediately following the `switch` itself. Looking at our example above, if `rate_class` were 2, the program would go directly to `case 2:`, calculate the cost, print out the value, then leave `switch` entirely.

The most general form of a `switch` statement is as follows:

```
      switch (<expression>)
        {
          case <value 1>:<statement 1>;
                      break;
          case <value 2>:<statement 2>;
                      break;
              ......
          case: <value n>:<statement n>;
                      break;
          default: <statement n+1>;
        }
```

The `break` Statement

Clearly, the place where execution of a `switch` statement begins depends on the value of the expression in the header. Where the execution *ends* is another matter. Once the program enters the body of a `switch` statement at a particular case value, it attempts to execute all subsequent statements of all cases. The purpose of the `break` statement is to cut off the execution after the selected `case` has finished. When a

Figure 3.4   Schematic diagram of the break statement.

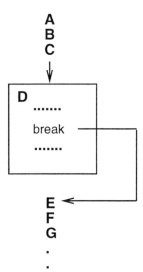

break is encountered, the program leaves the body of the switch statement, and proceeds to the statement immediately following switch. This is illustrated schematically in Figure 3.4. By placing a break at the end of each group of statements except the last, we ensure that one and only one **case** is executed.

From the above discussion, we might conclude that we should never leave out the break. This is not strictly true.

Example: **Different Case Values, Same Action**

For this code, case 1: and case 2: produce the same results:

```
switch (rate_class)
{
  case 1:
  case 2:
    cost = 22.3*(cars + bikes) + 26.1*trucks;
    printf("The cost for insurance is %f dollars \n", cost);
    break;
  case 3:
    cost = 22.3*(bikes + trucks) + 24.5*cars;
    printf("The cost for insurance is %f dollars \n", cost);
    break;
  default:
    printf("The class you have entered is invalid. \n");
}
```

If case 1: is selected, execution proceeds until the first break statement (which is after case 2:) is encountered. But this is clearly the same behavior as if case 2: had been selected.

Using the above scheme, we can force the same behavior on as many different **case** values as we like.

EXPERIMENT 3-4

(a) Suppose the selection requirements do not call for a default choice. Can the **default** keyword be left out?

(b) Could we have **case 10:** as a fourth choice in the example used in this section? Comment on this.

(c) Assuming a **default** choice is used, must it be the last one in the list?

Summary of Program 3.3

Strategy: Two new variables, **rate_class** and **bikes**, have been introduced in this program. The purpose of **rate_class** is to determine which formula is to be used to calculate insurance cost. The four variables—**cars**, **trucks**, **bikes**, and **rate_class**—are input using **scanf**. The value of **rate_class** determines which **case** of the **switch** statement is taken. In each **case**, the cost of insurance is calculated, then printed out.

Style:

- More than one **scanf** statement is used so that the number of items read in at one time is not large.

- The **case** keywords are indented with respect to **switch**; the statements of each **case** are uniformly indented with respect to **case**.

- A **default** case is provided even though it does essentially nothing. This alerts the programmer to situations where no **case** is processed.

Exercises

(3-12) Write this nested **if** statement as a **switch** statement:

```
if ((x == 1)  || (x == 2))
   printf("Fail \n");
 else if ((x == 3)  || (x == 4)  || (x == 5))
         printf("Satisfactory \n");
       else if ((x == 6)  || (x == 7))
               printf("Good \n");
             else if (x == 8)
                     printf("Great! \n");
```

(3-13) Simplify this **switch** statement:

```
switch (TooMany % 4)
    {
        case 0:printf("Very little. \n");
            break;
        case 1:printf("Not much more. \n");
            break;
        case 2:printf("OK. \n");
            break;
        case 3:printf("Great. \n");
            break;
        case 4:printf("Greater. \n");
            break;
        case 5:printf("Greatest. \n");
            break;
        case 6:printf("Really super! \n");
    }
```

(3-14) Simplify each of these selection statements.

```
if (x < 60)
  if (x > 75)
    printf("%d \n", x);
  else printf("%d \n", 2*x);
else printf("%d \n", 3*x);

if (x >= 60)
    printf("%d \n", x);
else if (x <= 50)
        printf("%d \n", 2*x);
    else if (x >= 70)
            printf("%d \n", 3*x);
        else printf("%d \n", 4*x);
```

(3-15) Redraw Figure 3.3 to illustrate the example entitled "Different case values, same action."

3.2

REPETITION

Repetition is accomplished using programming constructs known generically as *loops*. Although loops can be constructed three different ways in *C*, it is necessary for us to consider only two of them. As we shall see, these differ mostly in the way the computer determines when the repetition should cease. The process of repeating a given section of code is often called *iteration*. One complete pass over the section of code that is to be repeated is also called *an iteration*. A schematic diagram illustrating the general idea of a loop is shown in Figure 3.5.

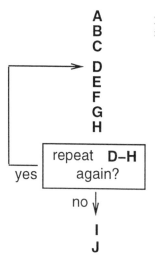

Figure 3.5   Schematic diagram illustrating the loop concept.

3.2.1 The `for` Loop

Suppose our hypothetical dealer wishes to know the cost of insurance for discount rates of 1%, 2%, etc., up to 10%. Clearly, a program that does this will repeat the same type of calculation ten times. In *C* the statement for this purpose is known as a `for` loop. It repeats a section of code a specified number of times. The exact number of repetitions is explicit in the statement of the loop itself.

Example: Using the `for` Loop to Repeat a Calculation

Consider line [1] of Program 3.4, which is a slight variation of one of our earlier themes.

```
for (counter = 1; counter <= 10; counter = counter + 1)
{
   discount = 0.01 * counter;
   total = (CAR_RATE * cars + TRUCK_RATE * trucks)*(1 - discount);
   printf("Cost = %f when discount = %d percent.  \n", total,
          counter);
}
```

The body is repeated ten times, each time with `1` added to the variable `counter`. Since `discount` depends on `counter`, and `total` depends on `discount`, ten different values of `total` are calculated. (A detailed look at this statement follows below.)

Let us look more closely at this statement. We view this as a header, followed by a body. The header consists of three expressions, all of which involve a *control variable*, in this case, `counter`, whose value determines whether or not the body executes. The body is everything between the two braces. Consider the header:

1. The first expression (`counter = 1`) is the *start rule* for the loop. It sets an initial value of the control variable. Here, the control variable `counter` starts at `1`.

2. The second expression (`counter` ≤ 10) is the *terminate rule* for the loop. This is a condition that must be met in order for the body of the loop to execute. In this example, the body of the loop will execute as long as the value of `counter` is not more than `10`. In effect, the second expression is a rule for terminating the repetition.

3. The third expression (`counter = counter + 1`) is the *increment rule* for the loop. This is a rule for updating the value of the control variable after each iteration. In the above example, `counter` is incremented by `1` after each iteration. Note that this happens automatically; the programmer does not insert a statement in the body of the `for` loop to update the control variable.

Let us now put the header together with the body and consider how the loop actually executes. First, `counter` is set to `1`. Immediately following this, `counter` is compared to `10`. Note that the comparison is made *before* the body of the loop is executed. If `counter` is no more than `10`, the three statements between the begin and end braces are executed. Then `counter` is incremented to `2`, and compared again to `10`. Since it is still no more than `10`, the three statements are executed again. After ten complete iterations, `counter` will be incremented to `11`. At this point, it is no longer true that `counter` ≤ 10. The iteration process halts, and the program continues with the statement following the `for`.

Example: **More `for` Loops**

```
(1) for (n = 0; n < 10; n = n + 1}
        {                           <- OK to use braces for only
        printf("%d \n", n*n);          one statement.
        }
(2) for (n = 0; n < 1; n = n + 1)
        prinf("%d \n", n);          <- Executes only once.
(3) for (n = 0; n < 5; n = n + 1)
        printf("Hello \n");         <- loop counter need not appear
                                       in body.
```

The general form of the `for` statement is as follows:

```
for (<start rule>; <terminate rule>; <update rule>)
  {
    <statement 1>;
    <statement 2>;
        ...
    <statement n>;
  }
```

There are no restrictions on the kinds of statements that comprise the body of the `for` loop. One can even use another `for` loop:

Example: **A Nested `for` Loop**

The following code writes `Hello` to the screen 50 times:

```
for (i = 0; i < 10; i = i + 1)
    for (j = 0; j < 5; j = j + 1)
        printf("Hello \n");
```

The *inner loop* (control variable `j`) is executed five times before the *outer loop* (control variable `i`) is incremented.

There is an abbreviated notation for the increment rule of a `for` loop. Instead of, say, `x = x + 1`, most *C* programmers write `x++`. We will follow this convention in all subsequent `for` loops. However, we will *not* use this substitution in any other circumstance until Chapter 10, when we discuss its consequences more thoroughly.

EXPERIMENT 3-5

    (a) Write a short program that includes a statement `n = n + 1` in the body of a loop (where `n` is the loop counter). Does the compiler allow this?

    (b) Can one use floating point numbers in the header of a **for** loop? Hint: Try something like `for (n = 1; n<5; n = n + 0.5)`.

    (c) Figure out what the notation `count--` means.

    (d) Run a short program that has this line:

```
for (n = 0; n < 10; n++);   /* note the semicolon! */
    printf("Hello \n");
```

Think carefully about what this code says, then try to explain what happened.

Summary of Program 3.4

Strategy: As in previous versions, the number of cars and trucks is read in. In the body of the `for` loop, a discount equal to one percent of the value of `counter` is applied to the value of `total`. Since `counter` varies from `1` to `10`, insurance costs discounted from one to ten percent are calculated and printed out.

Style:
- The body of the `for` loop is indented with respect to the header.
- The `for` loop is vertically separated from other statements in the program for readability.
- The programmer does not change the value of `counter` in the body of the loop.
- The loop counter is an integer value. (This is how we normally count things!)

- The value listed in the terminate rule—`10`—is numerically the same as the number of times the loop executes. This is useful to the programmer when troubleshooting. An equivalent rule in this case is `counter < 11`, but the `11` has no special significance, and does not remind the programmer how many times the loop is supposed to execute. If it were necessary to start the loop from `0`, but still execute ten times, then the rule `counter < 10` would be preferable to `counter ≤ 9`.

Exercises

(3-16) For each of these two code fragments, assume that the input is the following:

```
         5     1     -3     -8     -12
```

```
n = 50;
  for (k = 1; k <= 4; k++)
     scanf("%d", &x);
printf(%d \n", n+x);

n = 50;
for (k = 1; k <= 4; k++)
  {
    scanf("%d", &x);
    printf("%d \n", n+x);
    n = n - x;
  }
```

What is the output in each case?

(3-17) Will `total` contain the sum of all the integers from `7` through `25` after this code runs? Explain.

```
for (count = 7.0; count <= 25.0; count++)
   total = total + count;
```

(3-18) Will this code add all the even integers from `2` to `30`? Explain.

```
total = 0;
for (count = 1; count <= 15; count++)
   total = total + 2*count;
```

(3-19) Will this code print `clown` as many times as the user desires? (Assume `choice` is read in by the user)? Will it print `clown` at least once? Explain.

```
for (count = 1; count <choice; count++)
  {
    printf("clown \n");
    scanf("%d", &choice);
  }
```

(3-20) The goal of the following is to print all even integers between 2 and 14. Is that goal achieved? Explain.

```
for (i = 1; i <= 7; i++)
  {
    i = i + 1;
    printf("%d n", i);
  }
```

(3-21) What gets printed by this code?

```
for (i = -3; i <= 10; i = i - 1)
   printf("Watch out. \n");
```

(3-22) Suppose one types in this set of values at the `scanf` statement:

1 -2 -3 -4 -5 <return>

What is the output of this code:

```
sum = 0;
for (i = -5; i <= -1; i++)
   {
     scanf("%d", &data);
     sum = sum + data;
   }
printf("%d \n", sum);
```

(3-23) Given the following output:

4 6 8 10 12

What must the input be if the code that produced it is as follows

```
scanf("%d", &data);
for (count = data; count <= 2 * data; count++)
   printf("%d \n", 2 * count - data);
```

(3-24) Can the code of (3-23) produce output like this?

72 76 82 90 100 ...

Explain.

(3-25) Suppose one types these numbers at the keyboard when prompted for input: 3 4 5 6. What gets written out by the following?

```
scanf("%d %d %d", &a, &b, &c);
for (i = 1; i <= a; i++)
```

```
    {
      c = b - c;
      b = c;
      a = b + c;
      printf("%d \n", a);
    }
```

3.2.2 The `while` Loop

The `while` loop is used to repeat a section of code an indefinite number of times. The loop contains an explicit condition under which the repetition ceases, but one cannot predict by looking at the condition when that will happen.

Example: Using `while` to Repeat a Calculation

In Program 3.5, the `for` loop of Program 3.4 has been replaced by line [1], a `while` loop:

```
while (counter <= 10)
  {
    discount = 0.01 * counter;
    total = (CAR_RATE * cars + TRUCK_RATE * trucks)*(1 - discount);
    printf("Cost = %f when discount = %d percent.\n", total,
        counter);
    counter = counter + 1;
  }
```

As long as `counter` is no more than 10, the compound statement between the braces executes. (We go into more detail below.)

We can see immediately that the header of the `while` loop is much simpler than the header of a `for`. It contains only the equivalent of the `for` loop's terminate rule: the condition under which the body will execute. In our example, the control variable `counter` must be no more than 10 in order for the body to execute. As for the equivalent of the start rule and update rule, they are handled differently. The starting value of the control variable must be set *before* the loop is entered. The update rule must be set in the body of the loop; *it is not done automatically.* In this program, the starting value of 1 is set in the declaration of `counter`, while `counter` itself is incremented by 1 inside the loop.

The `while` loop works in the following way: Before the body of the loop executes, the value of the control variable `counter` is compared to 10. If `counter` is no more than 10, the body executes. After one pass through the loop the updated value of `counter` is rechecked; if it is still no more than 10, the body is executed again. This process continues until `counter` exceeds 10. Then the loop is exited, and the program continues with the statement that follows.

The general form of the `while` loop can be written this way:

```
while (<conditional expression>)
  {
    <statement 1>;
    <statement 2>;
        ...
    <statement n>;
  }
```

Example: **More `while` Loops**

```
(1) while (1)              <- Infinite loop!
      {
        <statements>
      }
(2) while (7)              <- Infinite loop.
      {
        <statements>
      }
(3) while (0)              <- Never executes.
      {
        <statements>
      }
```

Here are some important points about the `while` loop:

(**a**) The condition in the header is checked *first*. That is why, if it starts out with a value of `0`, the loop does not execute even once.

(**b**) One must always initialize the control variable of a `while` loop before the program gets to the loop. Otherwise, the program may behave in an unpredictable way.

(**c**) Always put a statement inside the loop that ultimately causes the conditional expression to change from *true* to *false*. Otherwise, the result will be an *infinite loop*, which is a loop that never stops repeating.

Count-Controlled versus Sentinel-Controlled Loops

Once the value of `counter` is set in Program 3.5, the loop will terminate after a definite number of repetitions. A loop that is constructed this way is known as a *count-controlled* loop. It is also possible to have a specific value, called a *sentinel*, terminate the loop:

Example: A Sentinel-Controlled Loop

Here, a value for the control variable is entered at the keyboard while the program executes.

```
while (doors != 9999)
  {
    printf("Enter the number of doors on this car:    ");
    scanf("%d", &doors};
  }
```

Since no car has 9999 doors, this would never be a valid input datum. Therefore, it is reasonable to look for 9999 as a signal to terminate. The value 9999
is the sentinel.

Note that even if we know the value of doors upon entry into the loop, we still can't
say how many repetitions there will be, since we can't predict the value of doors that
will be typed at the keyboard. Hence, this loop executes an indefinite number of
times.

EXPERIMENT 3-6

(a) Run this program (note the semicolon after the header):

```
counter = 5;
while (counter < 10);
   {
     printf("<a message> \n");
     counter++;
   }
```

What happened? Compare this behavior to that of the for loop with the
semicolon after the header.

(b) Run the same program except initialize counter to 15. What's the
difference here?

EXPERIMENT 3-7

Declare counter as a floating point number and write a short program with
these two statements:

```
counter = 0.0;
while (counter != 1.0)
   {
     counter = counter + 0.1;
     printf("%f \n", counter);
   }
```

Does the loop stop when counter is 1.0? Comment on the advisability of
using a real as the control variable.

Summary of Program 3.5

Strategy: Virtually the same as Program 3.4. The only difference is the use of
the while loop as opposed to a for loop. counter is initially set to 1; the loop termi-
nates after it executes with the value of counter set to 10.

Style:
- The body of the loop is indented with respect to the header.
- The loop counter is initialized before the loop is entered.
- The condition for loop termination indicates the number of times the loop should execute.

Exercises

(3-26) Change one line in this code so that the correct sum of the first 50 integers is printed out.

```
total = 0;
counter = 1;
while (counter < 50)
  {
    total = total + counter;
    counter = counter + 1;
  }
printf("%d \n", total);
```

(3-27) Do these two code fragments do the same thing? Explain.

```
counter = 3;
while (counter <5)
    while (counter > 2)
       counter = counter + 1;
printf("%d \n", counter);

counter = 3;
while ((counter <5) && (counter > 2))
   counter = counter + 1;
printf("%d \n", counter);
```

(3-28) Suppose we switch the order of the first of the above `while` loops:

```
counter = 3;
while (counter > 2)
  while (counter < 5)
    counter = counter + 1;
printf("%d \n", counter);
```

What is the result?

(3-29) Given these two lines of input:

```
4   8
6   2   3
```

What does the following code produce as output?

```
scanf("%d %d", &x, &y);
while (x < y)
  {
    x = y - 3;
    scanf("%d", &y);
  }
printf("%d \n", counter);
```

(3-30) What is the output of this code?

```
counter = 10;
y = 10;
while ((counter != 5)  || (y > 7))
  {
    printf("circus \n");
    counter = y - 3;
    y = counter + 2;
  }
```

(3-31) In the code of Problem 3-30, does the initial value of `counter` matter? Explain.

(3-32) Looking again at the code of Problem 3-30, what change could be made to the initial values of the variables to ensure an infinite loop?

(3-33) For each of the following, state whether the result is `always` an infinite loop, `sometimes` an infinite loop, or `never` an infinite loop. If the choice is `sometimes`, explain what the conditions are.

```
(a)  scanf("%d", &data);
     while (data < 7)
        printf("%d \n", data);
(b)  scanf("%d", &data);
     while ((data > 5)  || (data < 7) )
       {
         printf("%d \n", data);
         scanf("%d", &data);
       }
(c)  scanf("%d", &data);
     while ( (data > 5) && (data < 7) )
       {
         printf("%d \n", data);
         scanf("%d", &data);
       }
(d)  scanf("%d", &data);
     while ( (data < 5)  || (data > 7) )
        printf("%d \n", data);
```

```
(e)   scanf("%d", &data);
      while ( (data < 5)  || (data > 7) )
        {
         printf("%d \n", data);
         scanf("%d", &data);
        }
(f)   scanf("%d", &data);
      while ( (data < 5) && (data > 7) )
        printf("%d \n", data);
```

Programming Problems

(3-P1) Modify the menu program of Chapter 2 so that the user's choice of a menu selection results in a unique message being printed out.

User Input: An integer indicating a menu choice.

Program Output: One of these messages, depending on the user input as follows:

- Choice = 1: Message = Good Choice.
- Choice = 2: Message = Have a nice day.
- Choice = 3: Message = Change your oil.
- Choice = 4: Message = Cheers!

(3-P2) Modify the Celsius–Fahrenheit program of Chapter 2 so that the user has a choice of entering the temperature in Celsius or Kelvin.

User Input: (a) A floating point number denoting the temperature. (b) The character *C* or κ denoting the temperature system of the input.

Program Output: The statement The temperature of XX in SYSTEM1 is YY in SYSTEM2, where SYSTEM is replaced by the appropriate temperature system, and XX and YY are replaced by appropriate temperature values.

(3-P3) Modify the previous program (3-P2) so that after a temperature measurement is converted to Fahrenheit, the user can convert another temperature if so desired.

User Input: Same as for (3-P2) except that an input of 9999 causes the program to stop.

Program Output: The same as for (3-P2).

(3-P4) Modify the menu program of Chapter 2 so that the screen is cleared of the menu before the program outputs the message indicating the user's choice.

User Input: Same as for (2-P4).

Program Output: Same as for (2-P4).

(3-P5) Write a program that reads a line of keyboard input and counts the total number of vowels.

User Input: A line of text terminated with an asterisk.

Program Output: The statement `The total number of vowels in the line is YYY`, where `YYY` is the total number of vowels.

(3-P6) Write a program that converts five single digits (characters) to the number represented by those digits in reverse order.

User Input: Five single digits, type one per line.

Program Output: The number represented by the digits, last line first.

(3-P7) Write a program that prints out the quotient and remainder of an integer division.

User Input: Two integers: a dividend and a divisor.

Program Output: The statement `The quotient is QQQ and the remainder is RRR`, where `QQQ` and `RRR` are replaced by the quotient and remainder, respectively.

(3-P8) Write a program that exchanges the order of digits of a two-digit number.

User Input: A two-digit integer.

Program Output: The integer that results from reversing the digits.

(3-P9) Write a program that determines the number of digits that comprise a particular integer.

User Input: An integer.

Program Output: The statement `The number of digits in XXX is YYY`, with `XXX` replaced by the original integer, and `YYY` replaced by the number of digits.

PROGRAMS FOR CHAPTER THREE

Program 3.1: Selection Using an `if` Statement

```
#include<stdio.h>
  #define CAR_RATE      20.5
  #define TRUCK_RATE    31
  #define CREDIT        -25

  main()
   {
    int          cars, trucks;
    float        total;

    printf("Enter the number of cars, then the number of trucks");
    scanf("%d %d", &cars, &trucks);
    total = CAR_RATE * cars + TRUCK_RATE * trucks;

[1] if (cars > 50)      /* discount if cars exceed 50 */
       {
         total = 0.9 * total;
         printf("You qualify for a discount of ten percent. \n");
         printf("The stock exceeds the minimum by %d. \n", cars - 50);
       }

[2] printf("The insurance cost is %f dollars.", total + CREDIT);
   }
```

Program 3.2: Selection Using an `if-else` Statement

```
#include<stdio.h>
#define CAR_RATE      20.5
#define TRUCK_RATE    31
#define CREDIT        -25

main()
 {
  int          cars, trucks;
  float        total;
  printf("Enter the number of cars, followed by the number of
          trucks");
  scanf("%d %d", &cars, &trucks);
  total = CAR_RATE * cars + TRUCK_RATE * trucks;

[1] if (cars > 50)
     {
       total = 0.9 * total;
       printf("You qualify for a discount of ten percent. \n");
       printf("The stock exceeds the minimum by %d cars. \n",
              cars - 50);
     }
```

```
    else
      {
        printf("You do not qualify for a discount. \n");
        printf("The stock is below minimum by %d cars. \n",
               50 - cars);
      }

    printf("%f", total + CREDIT);
  }
```

Program 3.3: Selection Using a `switch` Statement

```
      #include<stdio.h>
      main()
        {
        int          rate_class;
        int          bikes, cars, trucks;
        float        cost;

        printf("Enter the rate class [1, 2, or 3]... ");
        scanf("%d", &rate_class);
        printf("Enter the number of bikes, cars, and trucks. \n);
        scanf("%d %d %d", &bikes, &cars, & trucks);

[1]     switch (rate_class)
          {
            case 1:
              cost = 22.3*(cars + bikes) + 26.1*trucks;
              printf("The cost for insurance is %f dollars \n", cost);
              break;
            case 2:
              cost = 24.5*(trucks + bikes) + 22.3*cars;
              printf("The cost for insurance is %f dollars \n", cost);
              break;
            case 3:
              cost = 22.3*(trucks + bikes) + 24.5*cars;
              printf("The cost for insurance is %f dollars \n", cost);
              break;
          default: printf("You have entered an invalid rate class. \n");
          }
        }
```

Program 3.4: Repetition Using a `for` Statement

```
      #include<stdio.h>
      #define CAR_RATE      20.5
      #define TRUCK_RATE    31
      #define CREDIT        -25

      main()
        {
        int          cars, trucks, counter;
        float        discount, total;
```

```
      printf("Enter the number of cars, then the number of trucks");
      scanf("%d %d", &cars, &trucks);     /* input statement */

[1]   for (counter = 1; counter <= 10; counter = counter + 1)
        {
          discount = 0.01 * counter;
          total = (CAR_RATE * cars + TRUCK_RATE * trucks)*(1 - discount)
                    + CREDIT;
          printf("Cost = %f when discount = %d percent.\n", total,
                  counter);
        }
      }
```

Program 3.5: Repetition Using a `while` Statement

```
#define CAR_RATE      20.5
#define TRUCK_RATE    31
#define CREDIT        -25

main()
  {
    int        cars, trucks, counter = 1;
    float      discount, total;

    printf("Enter the number of cars, followed by the number of
            trucks");
    scanf("%d %d", &cars, &trucks);    /* input statement */
[1]  while (counter <= 10)
       {
         discount = 0.01 * counter;
         total = (CAR_RATE * cars + TRUCK_RATE * trucks)*(1 - discount)
                       + CREDIT;
         printf("Cost = %f when discount = %d percent.\n", total,
                 counter);
         counter = counter + 1;
       }
  }
```

4 Functions

In this chapter, we will introduce one of the most important ideas in all of programming: the idea of a function. A function is a block of code that is given a name by the programmer. The *name*, not the actual code, is invoked in the program when the task represented by the code is needed. We describe this process by saying that the program *calls* the function; in this context, we refer to the program as the *caller*. Figure 4.1 illustrates a function call schematically. Execution of the main program is temporarily suspended after the execution of D, at which point the function begins executing. When the function finishes, execution of the main program resumes where it left off: immediately after D, at point E. Note that we have already encountered two functions that are part of the *C* library[1]: `scanf` and `printf`. We called these when our program required keyboard input and screen output, respectively.

We need to answer three main questions about functions:

1. How (and where) is a function defined?
2. How does the program call a function?

---

1 Appendix B describes some other useful library functions.

main program

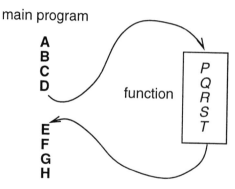

Figure 4.1   Schematic diagram of a function call.

3. How do we deal with *input* and *output*? In the context of functions, input refers to data that the caller must provide to the function before the function begins executing. Output refers to data produced by the function and returned to the caller.

Program 4.1 will help us start our exploration of functions. However, we will spend most of the time in this chapter examining Programs 4.2 and 4.3. Both do the same thing as Program 3.3, but their use of functions makes their overall design very different from that of Program 3.3.

4.1

FUNCTIONS: THE BASICS

Let us now answer the questions posed above. We begin with a function that involves neither input nor output. Although this is not a very realistic case, it illustrates some broad underlying ideas about functions. We will point out those characteristics of this case that are true in general.

Function Definition: Line [5] of Program 4.1 illustrates a function definition:

```
void print_message_1()
{
 printf("Use Table A to calculate rate for cars and bikes. \n");
 printf("Use Table B to calculate rate for trucks. \n");
}
```

All functions have a header (the first line) and a body (everything between the two braces). The first word in the header is always a keyword indicating the data type[2] of the output. In our case, the keyword is **void**, indicating that the function produces no output. For all functions, this keyword is followed by a name chosen by the programmer (here, **print_message_1**).

---

2 Called the "return type" of the function.

Next come a pair of parentheses. In this case, but not in general, the parentheses have nothing between them. This indicates that the function requires no input. For all functions, the body consists of the statements needed to perform the function's task. In this case, the task is simply to print some messages to the user.

Function Placement: The scheme for proper placement of the function definition is illustrated in lines [1]–[3], and line [5] of Program 4.1. First, a declaration very similar to a function header is placed prior to `main()`. Second, the code for the function itself is placed after the ending brace of `main`. The declarations in lines [1]–[3] are called *function prototypes*. The purpose of a prototype is to specify to the compiler the data types of the function's output and input. In our example, the `void` that precedes the function name tells the compiler what the function's output is (none, in this case). The `void` located between the parentheses tells the compiler that the function requires no input. We will have more to say about function prototypes at the end of the chapter.

Function Call: The proper method of calling a function depends on its input and output, or lack thereof.

> To call a function that involves no input or output, merely invoke its name, along with an empty pair of parentheses, followed by a semicolon.

In other words, use the function name *as if it were a statement*. This is illustrated in line [4] of Program 4.1, in the `switch` statement. Given a rate class of 1, 2, or 3, the program invokes the name `print_message_1()`, `print_message_2()`, or `print_message_3()`, respectively.

We close by noting the similarity between a function definition and the main program itself. This is no accident; `main()` is a function, too. (More about that later.) With that remark, we update our definition of a program: A C program is basically a series of declarations, followed by a series of functions, one of which must be called `main()`.

Summary of Program 4.1

Strategy: After reading in the values of `cars`, `trucks`, and `bikes`, and also `rate_class`, a `switch` statement calls one of three functions based on the value of `rate_class`. Each function simply prints out a message instructing the dealer to use a certain reference to calculate the insurance cost.

Style:
- The major tasks of the program are contained in the functions. The main program is basically a series of function calls.
- Each function is small (less than a half a page) and performs essentially only one task. This makes the function easy to debug.
- Each function definition is preceded by a comment describing briefly what the function does, and what its inputs and outputs are.

4.2

FUNCTIONS: INPUT AND OUTPUT

We now focus our attention on the types of functions that are most likely to be used in a program. When we are through with our discussion, we will be able to understand Programs 4.2 and 4.3 completely.

4.2.1 Functions with Input

Function Definition: In Program 4.2, there are three functions that involve input but no output. Let us consider the definition of one of them, line [5] (the other two are similar):

```
void print_rate_1(int x, int y, int z)
   {
     float rate;
     rate = 22.3*x + 22.3*y + 26.1*z;
     printf("The cost of insurance is %f \n", rate);
   }
```

Once again, the first word of the header is the keyword `void`, indicating that this function produces no output. However, the parentheses of this function contain a list of variable declarations. The variables in the list are the inputs to the function. Note that `x`, `y`, and `z` are used in the body seemingly without any assignment being made to them. We will explain this puzzle shortly.

We see in this program that it is possible to declare a variable (`rate`) within the body of a function. This is done when the variable is needed by the function, but not by the main program.

Lines [1]-[3] show the function prototypes. Once again, the `void` preceding the function name indicates that there is no output. What is new here is the list of type names between the parentheses. These are the type names of the inputs to the function; this is how the inputs to the function are described in a prototype.

Function Call: A call to the above function is shown in the `switch` statement (line [4]) of Program 4.2:

```
case 1: print_rate_1(bikes, cars, trucks);
case 2: ...
case 3: ...
```

As in the previous case, we make the call by invoking the function name, followed by a semicolon. However, in the present case, the parentheses are *not* empty. Instead, they enclose a list of three variable names, each of which is declared outside the function, and each of which has a value. Note that the data type of each of these variable names matches the respective type name in the prototype. Just prior to the start of `print_rate_1`, the value of `bikes` is assigned to `x`, the value of `cars` is assigned to `y`, and the value of `trucks` is assigned to `z`. Then `rate` is calculated, and its value printed out.

A Closer Look: The variables in the header of the function *definition* are known as the *formal parameters* of the function. The variables in the *call* of a function are known as the *actual parameters*. When a function is called, the values of the actual parameters are assigned to the formal parameters, with the *k*th formal parameter assigned the value of the kth actual parameter. This process is called *parameter passing.*

It is very useful for us to understand the underlying mechanism by which the parameters in the above example are passed. When the function `print_rate_1` is called [see part (b) of Figure 4.2], the system creates four *temporary* storage locations. Three of them are `x`, `y`, and `z`. The fourth is the variable `rate`. The value stored in `bikes` is copied into the temporary location `x`; the value stored in `cars` is copied into the temporary location `y`; the value stored in `trucks` is copied into the temporary location `z`. Then the statements of the function are executed, and a calculated value is stored in `rate`. This is the value that the function prints out. After the function has completed its execution [part (c) of Figure 4.2], all identifiers—`x`, `y`, `z`, and `rate`—become undefined. As we can see from the diagram, the data at those locations are not physically erased. However, they are no longer labeled by identifiers, so it is as if they don't exist at all. If the function is called again, new temporary locations for `x`, `y`, `z`, and `rate` are created, and the process begins anew.

Passing parameters to the function in the manner described above is known as *pass by value.* With this scheme, the *values* of `bikes`, `cars`, and `trucks`—copies of the contents of their locations—are passed to the function. *Since only copies of the actual parameters are used, their original values cannot be changed by any action of the function.*

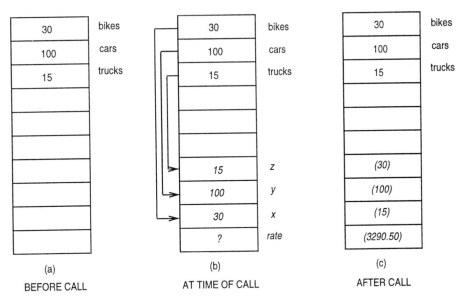

Figure 4.2 Schematic diagram of the memory before, during, and after a function call.

Summary of Program 4.2

Strategy: This is very similar to Program 3.3, except that values of `cars`, `bikes`, and `trucks` are passed to the appropriate function by the `switch` statement. Each function prints out the cost of insurance for each vehicle. The calculations are done in the `printf` statements.

Style: To avoid confusion and ambiguity, the formal parameters in the function definition have names that are different from the actual parameters passed to them.

4.2.2 Functions with Output

Function Definition: Program 4.3 has three examples of functions that return output to the caller. Line [5] shows one of them:

```
float calculate_rate_1(int x, int y, int z)
{
    float    rate;
    rate = 22.3*x + 22.3*y + 26.1*z;
    return(rate);
}
```

Let us concentrate on the differences between this and the function in the previous example. First, the header begins with the keyword `float`, rather than `void`. This indicates that the function returns a floating point value to the caller. Second, the statement `return(rate)` causes the function to return the value of `rate` to the caller. Note that the data type of `rate` is precisely that which is promised by the function's return type.

Lines [1]-[3] of Program 4.3 show the prototypes. Note that each of these declarations begins with `float`, indicating that the functions all return floating point numbers.

Function Call: The `printf` statements in line [4] of Program 4.3 illustrate how to call a function that returns output:

```
printf("Total cost is %f dollars \n", calculate_rate_1(bikes, cars,
        trucks));
```

As in the previous example, the function is called with the actual parameters substituted for the formal parameters. However, the function name is used *as if it were a variable name*. The entire expression `calculate_rate_1(bikes, cars, trucks)` is treated as a floating point variable by the `printf` function, and the value it returns gets printed out.

Examples: Function Calls

```
1. total = 2.5 * calculate_rate_1(bikes, cars, trucks);

2. if ( calculate_rate_1(bikes, cars, trucks) < 250.5 )
       total = 1.05 * total;
```

```
3. for (n = 1; n < 20; n++)
        printf("The cost for %d bikes is %f dollars \n",
                  calculate_rate_1(n, 0, 0));
```

A Closer Look: The underlying mechanism of this function call is very similar to the case previously described. When the function `calculate_rate_1` is called, four temporary locations—`x`, `y`, `z`, and `rate`—are created. The first three are assigned the values that are passed in, as described previously. The fourth, `rate`, is assigned a value during the course of the function's execution. After the function finishes executing, all four temporary locations cease to exist. Thanks to the `return` statement, however, the value of `rate` is preserved under the function name. That is, the expression `calculate_rate_1(bikes, cars, trucks)` evaluates to the value of `rate`, so the main program is able to print out this value.

EXPERIMENT 4-1

Consider the following function:

```
int    fun(int x)
  {
    int   z;
    z = x + 5;
    printf("%d is the value of z. \n", z);
  }
```

(a) Does the compiler let us get away without the `return` statement?

(b) Put in the statement `return(z)` just before the `printf`. Write any program that calls the function and prints its return value. What is the last statement to be executed in the function?

EXPERIMENT 4-2

(a) Is the expression `fun(5)` legal? That is, can we pass constants to the above function?

(b) Is it legal to pass an expression such as `3*5` to this function? How about `3*5 + 1`? And `3*5 + a`, where a is an integer?

(c) Write a short program with the function used like this: `fun(a)`; In other words, use `fun` as if it were a *statement*, not a variable. Does the compiler complain? Run the program. What happens to the value that `fun` returns?

(d) Write a short program that has two statements: any call to `fun`, followed by

```
printf("%f \n", z);
```

(In other words, try to print `z` from outside the function.) Why does the compiler report an error?

Summary of Program 4.3

Strategy: This is similar to the previous two programs except that here, the `printf` statements in `switch` call the calculation functions. Those functions are passed values of `cars,` `trucks,` and `bikes,` and calculate an insurance cost. Since each function is defined with a return type of `float`, each one returns a floating point value, which is then printed out.

Style: The variable `rate` is declared within the rate calculating functions, rather than external to those functions. That is because it is needed only within those functions, and not external to them.

Exercises

(4-1) What is the output of this program?

```
void one(int x)
{
    printf("The square of %d is %d \n", x, x*x);
}

main( )
{
    int a;
    a = 15;
    one(a);
}
```

(4-2) What is the output of this program?

```
void fun1(int a, int b)
{
    int z;
    z = b;
    b = a;
    a = z + b;
    printf("%d %d \n", a,b);
}

main( )
{
    int m,n;
    m = 3;
    n = 4;
    fun1(m,n);
    printf("%d %d \n", n,m);
}
```

(4-3) What is the output of this program?

```
void fun2(int a, int b)
{
   int x,w;
   w = a + b;
   x = b + w;
   printf("%d  \n", x);
}

main( )
 {
   int m,n;
   m = 3;
   n = 4;
   fun2(n,m);
   printf("%d %d \n", n,m);
 }
```

(4-4) What is the output of this program?

```
int increase(int x, int y)
{
  int n,z;

  for (n = 1; n < x; n++)
     y = y + n;
  z = y;
  return z;
}

main( )
 {
   printf("The answer is %d \n", increase(5,10));
 }
```

(4-5) Rewrite the % operation as a function.

(4-6) Draw a diagram similar to that of Figure 4.2 illustrating the call of the function `calculate_rate_1` of Program 4.3.

4.3

SCOPE

In Experiment 4-2 we saw explicitly that it is possible for a variable to be well defined in one part of a program, yet be undefined in another. In particular, a variable that was defined inside a function was inaccessible from the main program. The region of a program in which a given variable is defined is called the *scope* of that vari-

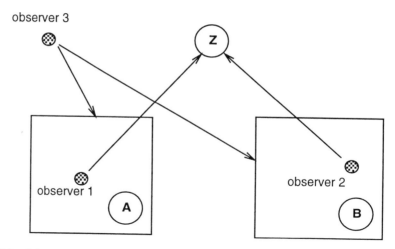

Figure 4.3 Schematic illustration of scope.

able. For our purposes, the following two ideas summarize what we need to know about scope:

- If a variable is declared in a function `f`, it is accessible inside `f`, but not outside `f`.
- If a variable is declared prior to the definition of all functions, including `main`, then it is accessible from anywhere in the program.

We can restate this using an analogy. Imagine a box made from one-way glass (Figure 4.3) such that someone outside can't see what's inside. However, someone inside the box can see what's outside. Hence, observers 1 and 2 in boxes `A` and `B` can see an object (`z`) outside their respective boxes. An observer outside these boxes cannot see inside either box, and cannot see object `A` or object `B`.

A C function is like the box. A variable defined inside the function (box) is inaccessible from the caller (can't be seen from outside the box). In Experiment 4-2, the variable `z` is defined in the box (function), and is therefore not accessible from the outside (main program). When the calling program tries to use it, the computer acts as if it doesn't exist.

A variable declared inside a function is called *local* to that function.[3] The variable `rate` in Program 4.2 is an example of a local variable. Local variables are accessible only from within the function where they are defined.

A variable declared before any functions are defined (not defined inside *any* box) is said to be *global*. Such a variable is accessible from anywhere in the program.

---

3 Usually, we just use the term *local*.

EXPERIMENT 4-3

(a) Compile a short program declaring an integer named p and a function named p. It looks like two things have the same name here! What does the compiler have to say about this?

(b) Compile a short program declaring a variable named x, and a function p that also declares a variable named x (same name!). Does the compiler accept this? Explain.

(c) Compile a short program declaring a variable named x, and a function p that has a parameter named x. Does the compiler accept this? Explain.

(d) Compile a short program that has function named p with a parameter named p. Does the compiler accept this? Explain.

(e) Compile a short program that has two functions, each with one parameter named x. Does the compiler accept this?

(f) Embellish part (b): instead of declaring an x in the program, declare a global x and initialize it to 5. Put these two lines in the program:

```
printf("%d \n", x);
p(x);
```

and these two in the function:

```
x = 8;
printf("%d \n", x);
```

Is it possible to write the value of the global x using the function's `printf` statement? Explain. Is a global variable always accessible within a function?

(g) Question: Suppose many people work on a huge program, with each responsible for a particular function. Should they be concerned that their choice of names for variables used in their functions will conflict with identical choices made by others?

4.3.1 Static Variables

In our discussions about parameter passing, we described how space for local variables is automatically allocated when the function in which they are declared executes, and deallocated when the function finishes. In C it is possible to declare a local variable that remains allocated even after the function finishes. The idea is to enable a function to have private access to a value that it produced during the previous call. The declaration is quite simple:

```
void    fun()
 {
   static int   x;
      ......
 }
```

The keyword `static` guarantees that `x` will remain allocated even after `fun` has finished executing. However, `x` is still local to `fun`; only `fun` can access it. The following experiment should make the behavior of a static variable clear.

EXPERIMENT 4-4

(a) Write a program that calls the function `fun(5)` three times:

```
void      fun(int y)
  {
    static int  x;
    x = x + y;
    printf("%d \n", x);
  }
```

Note the value printed out each time.

(b) Now change the `int  x` to `int  x = 5` and repeat the above. Does the initialization of `x` defeat the purpose of the static variable: to retain a value from the previous call?

Exercises

(4-7) Consider the skeleton of the program shown below, then answer the questions that follow it.

```
void    one(void);
void    two(int);
void    three(void);
int x,y;

main( )
  {
    < code for main program >
  }

void one()
  { int q,x;
    < code for function one >
  }

void two(int a)
  { int x;
    < code for function two >
  }

void three()
  {
    < code for function three >
  }
```

(a) Can the value of the global **x** be made available to function **one**? How about function **two**, and function **three**?

(b) If the main program makes this function call: **two(y)**; will a temporary location a be set up, with the contents of **y** copied into a?

(c) Since function **one** was declared before function **two**, can the value of **q** be made available to function **two**?

(d) Is it legal for the statement **y** = **x** to be made in function **one**?

(e) Would the statement **two(q)** in function **one** be legal?

(4-8) What is the output of this program?

```
void    fun1(int, int);
int m,n;

main( )
  {
    m = 3;
    n = 4;
    fun1(m,n);
    printf("%d %d \n", n,m);
  }

void fun1(int a, int b)
  {
    m = b;
    b = a;
    a = m + b;
  }
```

(4-9) What is the output of this program?

```
void    fun2(int, int);
int m,n;

main( )
  {
    m = 3;
    n = 4;
    fun2(n,m);
    printf("%d %d \n", n,m);
  }

void fun2(int a, int b)
  {
    a = m;
    n = b + a;
  }
```

4.3.2 The Function main( )

When we first introduced the topic of functions, we pointed out how a function looks quite a bit like a program. There is a good reason for that: What we had been calling a program up to that point—main—is in fact a function.

Since main is a function, we should be discussing the usual issues surrounding functions: definition, call, return value, and parameter passing. The "definition" is what we've been learning all along—how to write a program—and will continue to learn in forthcoming chapters. The "call" is made by the computer system when it executes the program. After the program is loaded into memory, control of the computer is passed to the function called main. Our main functions do not return anything; the warning that most compilers give reminds us of that. We will not concern ourselves with that issue, although the statement return (0) will eliminate the warning. As for parameter passing, we will leave this to Chapter 10 for readers who are curious. Clearly, given the way we have been writing **main,** no parameters have been passed to it.

4.3.3 A Note on Prototypes

A *function prototype* is a declaration that tells the compiler two things about a function:

- The return type of the function.
- The order and data type of the input parameters.

The compiler uses the function prototype to check the legality of subsequent function calls. If a prototype is left out, the compiler constructs a rather crude one of its own:

- The return type is assumed to be type int.
- No assumptions are made about the input parameters.

The consequences of this policy are explored in the next two experiments.

Experiment 4-5

Run the following program. Do not be deterred by the fact that there is no prototype, and that the function is called with two parameters despite being defined with only one. Note what happens.

```
#include<stdio.h>
main()
  {
    int a = 5;
    float b = 5.5;
```

```
    printf("%d \n", test(a,b));
}

int test(int x)
{
    int z;

    z = 2 * x;
    return(z);
}
```

In Experiment 4-5, the compiler makes the assumption that `test` returns an integer. For this case, that happens to be correct. Since no assumptions are made about the input parameters, the call to `test`, with two parameters, is considered acceptable. The result is that the compiler misses the incorrect function call, and we are left with output that we may or may not realize is in error.

EXPERIMENT 4-6

Change the definition of the function `test` in the previous experiment so that it returns `float`. Compile the program again. What happens?

In Experiment 4-6, the compiler again assumes that `test` returns a value of type `int`. However, when it encounters the actual definition of `test`, it sees `float` as the return type. This contradicts what the compiler "knows" about `test`; the definition is flagged as an error.

Programming Problems

Note: Each of these exercises requires that a function be written. The function should be tested out by a short program that calls the function and prints its output.

(4-P1) Write a function which converts all input times to seconds.

Function Input: Three integers: hours, followed by minutes, followed by seconds.

Function Output: The equivalent number of seconds.

(4-P2) Write a function that converts lowercase letters to uppercase letters.

Function Input: Any character.

Function Output: The uppercase version of that character if the input is one of the 26 letters of the alphabet, *or*, a question mark if the input is not a letter of the alphabet.

(4-P3) Write a function that rounds a number to the nearest 100.

Function Input: A real number.

Function Output: The integer multiple of 100 that is closest to the input.

(4-P4) Write a function that reverses the order of a three-digit number. Do this by calling another function that uses the code for programming exercise (3-P9) to reverse the digits of a two-digit number.

Function Input: A three-digit integer.

Function Output: The same integer with the digits in reverse order.

(4-P5) Write a program that adds the first *k* terms of the harmonic series

```
1/2 + 1/3 + 1/4 ....
```

Function Input: An integer denoting the number of terms in the series to add.

Function Output: The sum of the series up to that point (a real number).

(4-P6) Write a function that truncates a real number to an integer.

Function Input: A real number.

Function Output: An integer that is the input minus the fractional part.

(4-P7) Write a so-called *check digit* function.

Function Input: A six-digit number.

Function Output: An integer that is the one's digit of the sum of the input digits.

(4-P8) Write a function that calculates the cube of a number by calling another function that calculates the square.

Function Input: A real number.

Function Output: The cube of the input.

(4-P9) Write a function that converts a numerical grade to a letter grade.

Function Input: An integer in the range `0 - 100`.

Function Output: A character:

A: 90–100
B: 80–89
C: 70–79
D: 60–69
F: 0–59

PROGRAMS FOR CHAPTER FOUR

Program 4.1: Simple Function (No Input, No Output)

```
        #include<stdio.h>

[1]   void print_message_1(void);
[2]   void print_message_2(void);
[3]   void print_message_3(void);

      main()
        {
        int     rate_class, cars, trucks, bikes;

        printf("Enter rate class [1, 2 or 3] ...  ");
        scanf("%d", &rate_class);

        switch (rate_class)
          {
[4]         case 1: print_message_1();
                    break;
            case 2: print_message_2();
                    break;
            case 3: print_message_3();
                    break;
            default: printf("Case not on list. \n");
          }
        }

    /*  This function prints out two messages telling the user which
        tables to consult for insurance rates in class 1.

        Input: none.    Output: none.                          */
```

```
[5] void print_message_1()
     {
       printf("Use Table A for rates of cars and bikes. \n");
       printf("Use Table B  for rates of trucks. \n");
     }

  /*  This function prints out two messages telling the user which
      tables to consult for insurance rates in class 2.

      Input: none.         Output: none. */

   void print_message_2()
     {
       printf("Use Table A for rates of cars. \n");
       printf("Use Table C for rates of trucks and bikes. \n");
     }

/*  This function prints out two messages telling the user which
    tables to consult for insurance rates in class 3.

  Input: none.          Output: none.*/

  void print_message_3()
    {
      printf("Use Table B for rates of cars. \n");
      printf("Use Table A for rates of trucks and bikes. \n");
}
```

Program 4.2: Function with Input, But No Output

```
      #include<stdio.h>

[1]   void print_rate_1(int, int, int);
[2]   void print_rate_2(int, int, int);
[3]   void print_rate_3(int, int, int);

      main()
       {
        int    rate_class, cars, trucks, bikes;

        printf("Enter number of cars, then trucks, then bikes. \n");
        scanf("%d %d %d", &cars, &trucks, &bikes);
        printf("\n Enter rate class {1, 2, or 3] ...  ");
        scanf("%d", &rate_class);

        switch (rate_class)
           {
[4]         case 1: print_rate_1(bikes, cars, trucks);
                    break;
            case 2: print_rate_2(bikes, cars, trucks);
                    break;
            case 3: print_rate_3(bikes, cars, trucks);
                    break
```

```
                default: printf("Case value not in list \n");
            }

   /*  This function calculates and prints the cost of insurance
       for all vehicles based on rate class 1.

       Input: number of cars, trucks, bikes.   Output: none.  */

[5] void print_rate_1(int x, int y, int z)
      {
        float rate;
        rate = 22.3*x + 22.3*y + 26.1*z;
        printf("The cost of insurance is %f \n", rate);
      }

   /*  This function calculates and prints the cost of insurance
       for all vehicles based on rate class 2.

       Input: number of cars, trucks, bikes.   Output: none.  */

    void print_rate_2(int x, int y, int z)
      {
        float rate;
        rate = 24.5*x + 22.3*y + 24.5*z;
        printf("The cost of insurance is %f \n", rate);
      }

   /*  This function calculates and prints the cost of insurance
       for all vehicles based on rate class 3.

        Input: number of cars, trucks, bikes.   Output: none.  */

    void print_rate_3(int x, int y, int z)
      {
        float rate;
        rate = 22.3*x + 24.5*y + 22.3*z;
        printf("The cost of insurance is %f \n", rate);
      }
```

Program 4.3: Function with Input and Output

```
#include<stdio.h>

[1]  float calculate_rate_1(int, int, int);
[2]  float calculate_rate_2(int, int, int);
[3]  float calculate_rate_3(int, int, int);

   main()
   {
     int    rate_class, cars, trucks, bikes;

     printf("Enter number of cars, then trucks, then bikes. \n");
     scanf("%d %d %d", &cars, &trucks, &bikes);
```

```
           printf("\n Enter rate class [1, 2, or 3] ...   ");
           scanf("%d", &rate_class);
           switch (rate_class)
             {
[4]            case 1: printf("Total cost is %f dollars \n",
                            calculate_rate_1(bikes, cars, trucks));
               break;
               case 2: printf("Total cost is %f dollars \n",
                            calculate_rate_2(bikes, cars, trucks));
               break;
               case 3: printf("Total cost is %f dollars \n",
                            calculate_rate_3(bikes, cars, trucks));
             }
         }


     /* This function calculates the insurance cost for all vehicles
        based on rate class 1.

        Input: number of cars, trucks, bikes (integers).
        Output: total insurance cost (float).                   */

[5] float calculate_rate_1(int x, int y, int z)
      {
        float rate;
        rate = 22.3*x + 22.3*y + 26.1*z;
        return(rate);
      }

/* This function calculates the insurance cost for all vehicles
        based on rate class 2.

        Input: number of cars, trucks, bikes (integers).
        Output: total insurance cost (float).                   */

     float calculate_rate_2(int x, int y, int z)
       {
         float rate;
         rate = 24.5*x + 22.3*y + 24.5*z;
         return(rate);
       }

/* This function calculates the insurance cost for all vehicles
        based on rate class 3.

        Input: number of cars, trucks, bikes (integers).
        Output: total insurance cost (float).                   */

     float calculate_rate_3(int x, int y, int z)
       {
         float rate;
         rate = 22.3*x + 24.5*y + 22.3*z;
         return(rate);
       }
```

5 A Brief Introduction to Pointers

Program for Chapter Five

• Program 5.1: Function with address parameter

The idea of a pointer is also one of the most important in the *C* programming language. Many of the topics that follow in subsequent chapters are dependent on them. Unfortunately, pointers are also one of the most confusing topics for a beginning programmer. In this chapter, we will introduce the basic idea of a pointer variable, discuss how to declare them and assign values to them, and apply our new knowledge to a topic we recently covered: parameter passing.

5.1

THE POINTER CONCEPT

Suppose our friend Steve goes on vacation for three weeks and asks his neighbor Minna to feed his cat each morning. Needless to say, Minna can't do this unless she has a key to his house. Steve, known by his neighbors as a somewhat offbeat fellow, does not give her the key. Instead, he leaves her the following note:

Here's the combination to box **8000** at the post office. Inside you will find directions telling you where I keep my spare key.

We can say that instead of *directly* giving Minna the key to this house, Steve *indirectly* gives it to her by telling her where she can find it. If we were forced to describe this apparently foolish game in technical terms, we could say that Steve's post office box *points to* the location of his house key.

As it happens, we can do something analogous in a *C* program (although it will take a while to see that it is not a foolish game at all). Consider Figure 5.1, where we have drawn a schematic diagram of a hypothetical section of memory, arbitrarily chosen to be in the vicinity of location 8000. A variable x with value 35 is stored at address 8000. Another variable, p, whose *value* is 8000, is stored elsewhere. Up to now, we have been treating the contents of locations as an integer, a floating point number, or a character. Suppose, however, that we treat the contents of p in a special way: as a memory address. We could then say that p points to the variable x, since the value stored in p is numerically the same as the address of x. This gives us two ways to describe the 35 stored at location 8000:

It is the value of the variable x.

It is the value of the variable pointed to by p.

A variable whose data type is an address is called a *pointer*. The variable p of Figure 5.1 is therefore a pointer. Note that p has two addresses associated with it: the address where the variable p itself is stored, which is not of interest to us, and the address that p has as its value, which does interest us, since this is the place where p points.

Since memory addresses are seemingly like positive integer values, it is tempting to think that the contents of pointer variables are just like integers. One should not

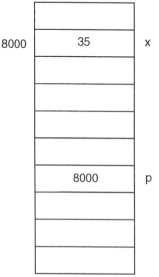

Figure 5.1   The variable p contains the address of the variable x. Hence, p points to x.

succumb to this temptation. It may be mathematically possible to perform an arithmetic operation on an address, but the result might very well have no meaning. For example, what does it mean to take the square root of an address? We will see later that there are some arithmetic operations that *can* be done on pointers, but only in special circumstances.

5.2

DECLARATION AND ASSIGNMENT OF POINTERS

The following is a simple example of a pointer declaration:

```
int     *p;
```

Were it not for the asterisk, this would be no different from an ordinary integer declaration that we have seen many times. The asterisk is the key, though. It means that p is a variable whose contents are treated as an address; i.e., p is a pointer. Indeed, the declaration as a whole says more: In essence, it is a promise that when p is assigned a value, that value will be the address of an integer.

There are four ways to assign a value to a pointer variable, three of which are described below[1] and illustrated in Figure 5.2. In part (a) of this diagram, p and q have been declared as pointers to type `int`, and `cars` has been defined as `25`.

1. Explicitly assign the address of another variable. Since the unary operator `&` can be used to give us the address of a variable, making an explicit assignment of an address to a pointer variable is quite easy:

```
p = &cars;
```

The effect of this assignment is illustrated in Figure 5.2(b): p points to `cars`.

2. Assign one pointer to another. Figure 5.2(c) shows the effect of assigning p to q: q is set to point to the same place pointed to by p.

EXPERIMENT 5-1

Declare a pointer, p, to an integer, and another, q, to a character. Is it possible to get p to point to the same variable as q?

3. Assign a predefined constant called NULL. In Figure 5.2(d), NULL has been assigned to the pointer q. This avenue for pointer assignment is a special case. There are times when we would like a pointer variable not to point anywhere in particular. A pointer whose value is NULL is treated this way.

---

1 The fourth method will be discussed in Chapter 6.

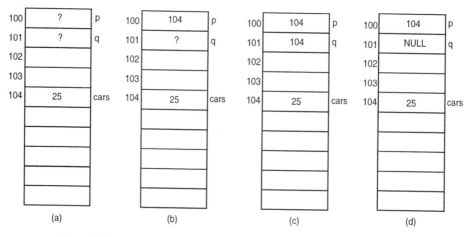

Figure 5.2   Assigning values to pointers.

5.2.1 The Dereferencing Operator

At the outset of this chapter, we said that the asterisk denotes the fact that p is a pointer. Actually, the asterisk is a unary operator called the *dereferencing*[2] operator. Dereferencing means accessing the value pointed to by a pointer. When used in front of a pointer name, the combination of asterisk and pointer refers to the quantity pointed to by the pointer. This is a very important idea, which we summarize as follows:

If p is the address of a variable v, then *p and v refer to the same quantity.

---

2 It is also extremely important not to confuse the asterisk in this context (operator is *unary*, operation is *dereference*) with the asterisk we used before pointers were introduced (operator is *binary*, operation is *multiply*).

The variables *p and `cars` of Figure 5.2(b) are the same thing. It is extremely important to realize, however, that until p is actually assigned the address of something, the quantity *p is meaningless. However, it is not undefined; so an accidental reference to it will not be flagged as an error by the compiler. In the next experiment, we look into this.

EXPERIMENT 5-3

Write a program that declares p, q, and r as pointers to an integer, a floating point number, and a character, respectively. Add this statement:

```
printf("%d %f %c \n", *p, *q, *r);
```

Note that this compiles without error, which verifies the fact that *p, *q, and *r at least exist. Run the program. How can we explain the values that are output? After all, we didn't point p, q, or r anywhere, nor did we assign anything to *p, *q, and *r!

5.3

PASSING POINTERS TO FUNCTIONS

Let us now look at a practical use of the pointer concept. We have modified the three functions of Program 4.2, along with the statements in `switch`. The result is Program 5.1. Note that in this program, the answer we want is in a variable called `rate`, which gets printed out in the `switch` statement. However, it appears that `rate` is never assigned a value in `main`, and it is certainly not returned by the `calculate_rate` functions, since their return type is `void`. In this section, we will show that these function calls in effect assign a value to `rate`.

Function Definition: The `calculate_rate` functions of Program 5.1 (line [5]) illustrate how to define a function where one of the parameters is a pointer:

```
void calculate_rate_1(int x, int y, int z, float *r);
{
    *r = 22.3*x + 22.3*y + 26.1*z;
}
```

Again, let us concentrate only on those aspects of this function definition that differ from what we have seen previously. First, the declaration `float *r` means that r is a pointer to a floating point number. Second, in the body of the function, the calculation involves the number itself, *r, not the pointer, r.

Note the function prototypes (lines [1]-[3]). The correct data type notation for a pointer is the type to which it points, followed by the asterisk.

Function Call: The call to the above function is shown in the `switch` statement, line `[4]`:

```
switch (rate_class)
    {
      case 1:  calculate_rate_1(bikes, cars, trucks, &rate);
          . . . . . . . . . . .
    }
```

Since this function does not return a value, we use it by invoking its name, followed by a semicolon. More important, since the fourth parameter is a pointer, we pass in the address of `rate` rather than the value of `rate`. We generalize this important idea as follows:

If a formal parameter is a pointer, the corresponding actual parameter must be an address.

Example: Function Call

If `ptr` is declared as a pointer to type `float`, we can also call the above function this way:

```
calculate_rate_1(bikes, cars, trucks, ptr);
```

A Closer Look: The big question is, *How does* `rate` *get assigned a value?* We can answer this question with the aid of Figure 5.3. When `calculate_rate_1` is called (Figure 5.3b), the computer creates the following temporary locations: one for `x`, one for `y`, one for `z`, and one for `r`. No temporary location is created for `*r`. In-

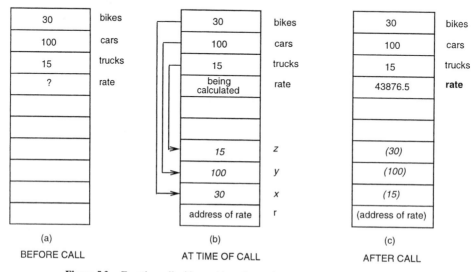

Figure 5.3   Function call with an address (`&rate`) parameter.

stead, the address of `rate` is copied into `r`. *The actual location `rate` is used for the calculation.* It is as if the line in the function were written like this:

```
rate = 22.3*x + 22.3*y + 26.1*z;
```

Since the actual location of `rate` is used, and not merely a copy of its contents, `rate` itself is changed by the action of this function. Thus, when `calculate_rate_1` finishes, it leaves the desired answer in `rate`.

Passing addresses as parameters is known as *pass by reference*, so called because a reference to a location, rather than a copy of a value, is the quantity passed. The location that is used is precisely the one pointed to by the pointer that is passed in. *Since the function does its manipulations at the actual locations of the variables that are passed by reference, those variables are liable to be changed by the function.*

EXPERIMENT 5-4

Write a short program using one of the `calculate_rate` functions and call it like this:

```
calculate_rate_1(10, 10, 10, 10);
```

Explain the result.

Let us now summarize what we know about the essentials of parameter passing. Parameters are avenues for communication between a function and its caller. Parameters used in the definition of a function are called *formal parameters;* those used in the call of a function are called *actual parameters.* The caller provides input to the function by passing actual parameters to the corresponding formal parameters.

There are two ways to pass parameters: pass a copy of the parameter (pass by value), or pass the address where the parameter is located (pass by reference). The method of pass by reference has two implications: constants cannot be passed as parameters, and the input data are liable to be changed by the actions of the function. With pass by value, the opposite is true in both cases: input data cannot be changed by the function, but constants can be passed.

Summary of Program 5.1

Strategy: As in the Chapter 4 programs, values of `cars`, `trucks`, and `bikes` are passed into a function for the purpose of calculating an insurance cost. In this case, however, the address of a variable called `rate` is also passed in. Each function stores the result of its calculation in `rate`, a variable defined in the main program. By the time any of the `printf` functions is called, `rate` has been calculated, and can be printed out.

Style: No additional points in this program.

Exercises

(5-1) Assume these declarations in a program:

```
int      a = 7;
float    b = 7.0;

void test(int x, float *y)
```

Are the following statements legal in a main program?

```
(a)      test(7,7);
(b)      test(7,7.5);
(c)      test(a, &b);
(d)      test(b, a);
(e)      test(a, a);
```

(5-2) What is the output of this program?

```
void     fun3(int *);

main( )
  {
      int  a;

      a = 4;
      fun3(&a);
      printf("%d \n", a);
  }

void fun3(int *x);
  {
      int  a,b;
      a = *x + 5;
      b = *x - 3;
      *x = a * b;
  }
```

(5-3) What is the output of this program?

```
void     fun4(int, int *);

main( )
  {
      int  b,x;

      a = 5;
      b = 2;
      fun4(a,&b);
      printf("%d %d \n", b, a);
  }
```

```
void fun4(int x, int *y)
 {
    int   a,b;

    a = x + *y;
    x = a - *y;
    *y = x - a;
 }
```

(5-4) Redo Exercise (4-5) using pass by reference.

(5-5) What is the output of this program?

```
void      fun1(int, int *);
void      fun2(int *, int);

main( )
 {
    int   a,b;
    a = 4;
    b = 2;
    fun2(&a,b);
    printf("%d %d \n", a, b);
    fun1(a,&b);
    printf("%d %d \n", a, b);
 }

void fun1(int x, int *y)
 {
    *y = abs(x - *y);
 }

void fun2(int *x, int y)
 {
    int a,b;
    a = *x + 5;
    b = y - a;
    *x = a - b + y;
 }
```

(5-6) What is the output of this program?

```
void      fun3(int, int *);
void      fun4(int, int *);

main( )
 {
    int   a,b;

    a = 4;
    b = 2;
    fun3(a,&b);
    printf("%d %d \n", a, b);
```

```
        fun4(a,&b);
        printf("%d %d \n", a, b);
    }

void fun3(int x, int *y)
{
    *y = abs(x - *y);
}

void fun4(int x, int *y)
{
    int a,b;

    a = x + 5;
    b = *y - a;
    x = a - b + (*y);
}
```

Untyped Pointers

All the pointers we have used up to now have been declared as pointers to a specified data type. The computer needs the type so that it can properly dereference the pointer. There are times, however, when it is not appropriate for a pointer to have a type associated with it. For example, we may not be interested in dereferencing a particular pointer p. Instead, we just want p to serve as a temporary storage location for (possibly) different kinds of pointers. Also, we will soon encounter a function that returns an untyped pointer. We can declare an untyped pointer as follows:

```
    void     *p;
```

This declares p as a pointer to any data type. We say that p is an *untyped* pointer. A pointer of any type may be assigned to p. Conversely, p can be assigned to any type of pointer.

Programming Problem

(5-P1) Write a program that reads ten integers from the keyboard, stores them in the memory using pointer arithmetic, then calculates the average of the numbers.

User Input: Ten integers.

Program Output: A statement `the average of the ten numbers is XX.`, where XX is replaced by the average of the ten numbers.

The remaining programming assignments for this chapter are identical to those of the preceding chapter *except* that the return type of each function must be changed to `void`. Thus each function must be rewritten so that addresses are passed, and parameters are used as avenues of output.

PROGRAM FOR CHAPTER FIVE

Program 5.1: Function with Address Parameter

```
        #include<stdio.h>

[1]   void calculate_rate_1(int, int, int,  float *);
[2]   void calculate_rate_2(int, int, int,  float *);
[3]   void calculate_rate_3(int, int, int,  float *);

      main()
      {
        int   rate_class, cars, trucks, bikes;
        float   rate;

        printf("Enter the number of cars, then trucks, then
               bikes.\n");
        scanf("%d %d %d", &cars, &trucks, &bikes);
        printf("\n Enter the rate class [1, 2, or 3] ...");
        scanf("%d", &rate_class);

        switch (rate_class)
          {
[4]         case 1: calculate_rate_1(bikes, cars, trucks, &rate);
                    printf("Total cost is %f dollars \n", rate);
                    break;
            case 2: calculate_rate_1(bikes, cars, trucks, &rate);
                    printf("Total cost is %f dollars \n", rate);
                    break;
            case 3: calculate_rate_1(bikes, cars, trucks, &rate);
                    printf("Total cost is %f dollars \n", rate);

          }
      }

   /* This function calculates the cost of insurance for all
      vehicles base on rate class 1.

      Input: number of cars, trucks, bikes (integers, pass by value)
             insurance cost (float, pass by reference)

      Output: none.                                              */

[5] void calculate_rate_1(int x, int y, int z, float *r)
       {
           *r = 22.3*x + 22.3*y + 26.1*z;
       }

   /* This function calculates the cost of insurance for all
        vehicles base on rate class 2.

        Input: number of cars, trucks, bikes (integers, pass by value)
               insurance cost (float, pass by reference)
```

```
          Output: none.                                              */

     void calculate_rate_2(int x, int y, int z, float *r)
        {
           *r = 24.5*x + 22.3*y + 24.5*z;
        }

/* This function calculates the cost of insurance for all
        vehicles base on rate class 3.

        Input: number of cars, trucks, bikes (integers, pass by value)
               insurance cost (float, pass by reference)

        Output: none.                                              */

     void calculate_rate_3(int x, int y, int z, float *r)
        {
           *r = 22.3*x + 24.5*y + 22.3*z;
        }
```

6 Arrays

So far, the data types we have met have been easy to handle. For example, variable declarations have been nothing more than the simple mention of a keyword such as `int`. The computer "knows" exactly what we mean, and reserves a fixed amount of space for it. Now we move on to what are generally called *data structures*: data that can be broken down into smaller components, each of which is a recognizable data type. In this chapter, we will look at a data structure known as an *array*: its components are all of the same data type. As we discuss arrays, we will try to answer the following questions:

1. What sorts of quantities can be represented by arrays?
2. How do we declare array variables?
3. How do we distinguish between the entire array and a single component of an array?
4. What is the relationship between pointers and arrays?
5. What are the rules about passing an array as a parameter to a function?

month	mean temperature
SEP	62.5
OCT	55.2
NOV	47.1
DEC	31.5
JAN	29.8
FEB	27.7
MAR	38.6
APR	48.8
MAY	61.5
JUN	73.3

Figure 6.1   A simple table of values.

6.1

ONE-DIMENSIONAL ARRAYS

The first of the above questions is easy to answer. A *one-dimensional array* is used to represent any quantity whose value depends on a single discrete variable. Such quantities abound in the everyday world; an example is shown in Figure 6.1. Here, the mean monthly temperatures for a particular school year are summarized in a neat table. The value of temperature depends on a single variable: the identity of the month. Some other examples are:

(a) The batting averages of all players on a team. The batting average depends on the identity of the player.

(b) The seating capacity of all rooms in the science building on campus. The number of seats depends on the room.

(c) The number of different types of vehicles in a used car dealership inventory. The number of vehicles depends on the vehicle type (bike, car, truck).

The next two questions are answered by examining Program 6.1. This is essentially the same as Program 4.2 except that it uses a single one-dimensional array, rather than three separate variables, to represent the entire vehicle stock of our dealer.

Example: Declaring a One-Dimensional Array

A one dimensional array is declared in line [4] of Program 6.1:

```
int     vehicle[3];
```

The visible difference between this and an ordinary integer declaration is the 3 surrounded by a pair of square brackets. The identifier `vehicle` by itself is the name of the array. The keyword `int` signifies that each element of the array is an integer. The 3 inside the square brackets denotes the number of elements in the array (also called the *dimension* of the array). The quantity `vehicle` is therefore an array of three integers.

Examples: **Declaring One Dimensional Arrays**

Possible array declarations for the three lists described at the outset of this section are:

```
float        temperature[31];
float        batter[25];
int          roomsize[40];
```

Example: **Denoting a Single Element of an Array**

The comment following the declaration of the integer array (line [4]) illustrates the scheme for identifying an element of an array:

```
vehicle[0]
```

In general, we denote an individual element of an array by the array name followed by square brackets, which enclose an integer. The integer is an index, starting with 0, which denotes the desired element. Thus `vehicle[0]` is the first of the three elements of this array.

Example: **Accessing All the Elements of an Array**

The `for` statement (line [5]) in Program 6.1 also illustrates a common method for accessing all the elements of an array:

```
for (n = 0;  n < 3;  n++)
    scanf("%d", &vehicle[n]);
```

As n varies from 0 to 2, the `scanf` function reads the value of the corresponding element of `vehicle` from the keyboard.

Examples: **Statements with Array Variables**

```
(1) if ( vehicle[n] < smallest )
        smallest = vehicle[n];          <- Loop finds smallest element.

(2) if ( vehicle[n] > largest )         <- Loop finds largest element.
        largest = vehicle[n];

(3) for ( n = 1; n < 3; n++ )           <- Note starting index!
      {                                    Smallest array index
        scanf( "%d", &x[n] );              can't be less than 0.
        x[n] = n * x[n-1];
      }
```

As with scalar variables, we can initialize an array right in the declaration: We simply use braces to surround a list of values. For example, suppose we knew that there were 10 bikes, 15 cars, and 32 trucks. Then our declaration of `vehicle` could be made this way:

```
int vehicle[3] = { 10, 15, 32 };
```

When initializing an array in the declaration, we can leave off the dimension:

```
int vehicle[] = { 10, 15, 32 };
```

The compiler will determine that there are three elements in this array.

We can summarize the rules for declaring a one-dimensional array as follows:

```
<type name>  <variable name>[<dimension>] = {<value list>};
```

We can leave off the dimension, or we can leave off everything to the right of the square brackets. However, we can't leave off both. Note that it would be impractical to initialize the arrays `temperature`, `batter`, or `roomsize` in the declaration; there are too many items in each to list conveniently.

Summary of Program 6.1

Strategy: Identical to that of Program 4.3, except that instead of passing `cars`, `bikes`, and `trucks` as three separate parameters, a single array parameter is passed. We elaborate on this in Section 6.2.2.

Style:

• Instead of hard coding the size of the array into the program, a symbolic constant is used. That makes changing the size of the array easy: just change the value of the constant.

• The elements of the array are initialized before they are used.

• In the `for` loop, the terminate rule is expressed as `n < SIZE` to ensure that the array index does not go out of range, and to remind the programmer how many elements there are in the array. In this case, for example, `n <= 2` is an equivalent rule, but it does not suggest anything about the array size.

6.2

ARRAYS AND POINTERS

What exactly does it mean when we say that `vehicle` represents the entire array? Let us try to determine the answer with a simple experiment.

EXPERIMENT 6-1

In this experiment we will attempt to determine the data type of an array name. Run a program that has the following lines:

```
int    vehicle[] = {10,20,30};
printf("%u %u \n", vehicle, &vehicle[0]);
```

(Recall that the format specifier **%u** is used to output unsigned integers such as addresses.) How do the two values output by the **printf** compare? (The actual values are not important.) What can we conclude about the data type of **vehicle**?

From the output of the **printf** of the experiment, we can conclude that **vehicle** and **&vehicle[0]** are the same thing. Since **&vehicle[0]** is clearly an address, **vehicle** must also be an address, namely, the address of the first element of the array! This is illustrated in Figure 6.2. Note that there are two main parts to the diagram: a contiguous block of memory, and a separate place reserved for the identifier **vehicle**. The contiguous block is the actual array of three integers; **vehicle** is simply a pointer to the beginning of this array. (The arrow, by the way, is a convenient way of indicating that something is a pointer, and showing where it points.) In the next experiment, we will learn a little more about this pointer.

EXPERIMENT 6-2

Consider the array **vehicle**. Certainly we can negate all its elements with a statement like this:

```
for (n = 0; n < 3; n++)
        vehicle[n] = - vehicle[n];
```

We could, in fact, perform any given modification on all the elements of **vehicle** using the above loop. The question is, can we modify the array as a whole without looping through it element by element? Test out this idea by trying to negate the entire array with the statement **vehicle = - vehicle**. Would a similar statement involving another operation, such as **vehicle = 2 * vehicle**, work any better?

In the above experiment, we tried to modify the entire array with a statement like this:

```
vehicle = <something>
```

The reason we were not successful is that the array name, **vehicle**, is a *constant*, and hence can't be changed. There is no *variable* that explicitly denotes the entire array; **vehicle[n]** and ***vehicle** denote single elements, while **vehicle** is a constant. Since there is no such variable, it is not possible to change the array as a whole. The only way to modify all the elements of an array is to do it element by element.

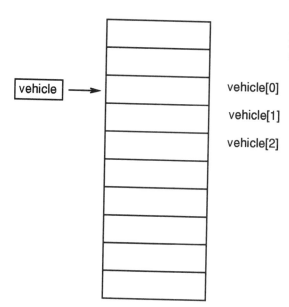

Figure 6.2 Schematic diagram illustrating the representation of an array in memory.

vehicle[0]

vehicle[1]

vehicle[2]

6.2.1 Pointer Arithmetic

In this section we will see explicitly why addresses cannot be thought of as ordinary integers. The first thing we need to do is establish some rules about which arithmetic operations on pointers are allowed, and which are not. We can do this with a simple experiment.

EXPERIMENT 6-3

Make these declarations:

```
int     *p, *q;
```

Test the legality of the following arithmetic expressions (just compile them):

```
p + q;  p - q;  p * q;  p / q;  p + 3;  p - 3;  p * 3;  p / 3;
```

Make a list of which ones are legal. Then test the validity of these relational expressions:

```
p == q;  p > q;  p < q;  p != q;  p <= q;  p >= q;
```

Again, simply note which are legal.

In the experiment above, we discovered that not all arithmetic operations on pointers are legal. It is possible only to add an integer to a pointer, subtract an integer from a pointer, and subtract one pointer from another. What is the significance of these operations? Let's try to find out by doing another experiment.

EXPERIMENT 6-4

Declare the following variables:

```
int     vehicle[] = {10, 20, 30};
int     *p, a = 15;
```

and execute these statements:

```
p = vehicle;
printf("%d %d %d \n", vehicle[1], *(p+1), p[1]);

p = &a;
printf("%d %d %d \n", p[0], *(p+1), p[1]);
```

Note that p is not defined as a pointer to an array, yet the notation p[n] is accepted by the compiler. Record the values that are output. We discuss the results below.

Pointer ± Integer: Let's start by noting that the outputs from the first `printf` statement are all the same. Does this mean that the variables in this `printf` are all the same object? We can easily recognize `vehicle[1]` as the second element (`20`) of the array, but what about the other two? They are also the same. To appreciate why, let us reconsider a typical array `A`, and ask ourselves *Where is element `A[n]` located?* The answer depends on the size of an element. If an element occupies `k` bytes in memory, then element `A[n]` is `k * n` bytes from the beginning of the array. Since the size of an element is known to the computer as a consequence of the type declaration, only the beginning of the array and the value `n` need be specified. Since `A` points to the beginning of the array, the expression `A[n]` clearly has all the information needed to locate element `n`. But any pointer `p` to the beginning of the array conveys the same information as `A`. Thus `p[n]` should be just as good as `A[n]`

The expression `*(p+n)` is simply an alternative expression for `p[n]`. Here is the reason why: In Experiment 6-4, `vehicle` is an array of integers as shown in Figure 6.3a. Since `p` is set equal to `vehicle`, `p` points to the first integer of the array, `vehicle[0]`. Now, from the previous discussion, we know that `(p+1)` points one integer beyond the beginning; so `*(p+1)` must be the second element in the array. That is, `*(p+1)` is `p[1]`. Extending this reasoning, we can see that `*(p+n)` and `p[n]` are the same quantities.

Now consider the outputs from the second `printf`. The expression `p[0]` is `0` bytes from the beginning of the address of `a`, which explains why the output is `a` itself, `10`. But what about the value output for `*(p+1)`? It is treated as an integer located one integer's worth of memory beyond `a`. However, as we can see from Figure 6.3(b), we don't know what is stored there. Hence, the quantity `*(p+1)` (or `p[1]`) is

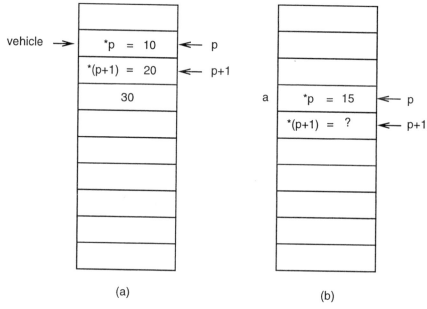

Figure 6.3   Memory setup for pointer arithmetic.

not meaningful. This underscores an important point: The addition (or subtraction) of an integer and a pointer is meaningless unless it is done on arrays. An expression such as p±n always points to a block of memory some distance away from p. If p points to an element of an array, then meaningful data exist between p and p±n, since the elements of an array are contiguous. Of course, this assumes that n is such that it does not take us beyond the bounds of the array.[1] If p points to something other than an array, then we can't be sure of what's beyond *p.

Difference between Two Pointers: Let us assume that p and q point to an element type that occupies k bytes in memory. Then p - q is simply the number of blocks of memory of size k bytes lying between those two addresses. But what exactly lies between *p and *q? We can't say with certainty unless both pointers point somewhere in the same array. The contiguous storage property of arrays ensures that the intervening data are meaningful.

Relational Operations on Pointers: We must also be careful when using relational operations on pointers. Suppose two pointers point to the same array. Then we could compare the values of the two pointers to determine which one points to a higher element number. However, if the pointers don't point to the same array, such a comparison is meaningless. Figure 6.4 shows a case where p > q, yet p points near the beginning of an array, while q points near the end.

---

1 Exceeding the bounds is possible, and will almost always produce erroneous results.

Figure 6.4 More pointer arithmetic (see text).

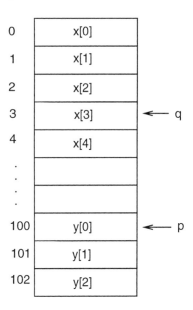

6.2.2 Passing Arrays as Parameters

In Program 6.1 a single array identifier is used in place of three separate identifiers to represent the three types of vehicles in the dealer's inventory. The heart of the calculation in this program is the passing of this array to a function that calculates the insurance cost. Note that the rules for passing a one-dimensional array are the same regardless of the dimension of the array; so we can generalize from the three element situation we have here.

Function Definition: The function `calculate_rate_1`, shown in line `[7]` of Program 6.1, has a single array as its formal parameter:

```
float calculate_rate_1(int v[]);
{
  float rate;
  rate = 22.3*v[0] + 22.3*v[1] + 26.1*v[2];
  return(rate);
}
```

Except for the header, this follows all the rules for defining a function that returns a value. The header is puzzling, though: The array name is specified, but without any dimension. Is it possible that the function does not need the size of the array that will be passed to it? As we will discover shortly, the size doesn't matter.

Lines `[1]`–`[3]` are the function prototypes. The correct way to specify a one-dimensional array in a prototype is to write the element type followed by a pair of empty braces.

Function Call: The call to the function `calculate_rate_1` is found in the `switch` statement, line `[6]` of Program 6.1:

```
printf(" ... ", calculate_rate_1(vehicle));
```

Note that the actual parameter (`vehicle`) is a pointer; so it need not be preceded by the `&` to be turned into an address.

A Closer Look: In order for a function to deal successfully with an array parameter, it needs to be able to calculate the address of any element of the array that is passed to it. Such a calculation involves determining the number of elements between element `i` and the beginning of the array. We have already done most of the work for this problem. Recall that if each element occupies `k` bytes, then the element indexed by `i` is `k * i` bytes from the beginning of the array. Hence:

```
address of x[i] = starting address + k * i
```

The array name provides the starting address, the index `i` is specified in the element identifier `x[i]`, while the number of bytes per element is implicit in the type declaration. Clearly, the array dimension is not required for the calculation, so it does not have to be specified in the header.

EXPERIMENT 6-5

Suppose we mistakenly declare an array this way:

```
int    x[5] = {22, 4, 16, -9};
```

What does the computer do about the missing fifth element? On the other hand, suppose the mistake is like this (an extra element):

```
int    x[5] = {22, 4, 63, 9, 0, 12};
```

What happens?

EXPERIMENT 6-6

(a) Suppose a variable `x` is declared as an array of dimension 5, so that `x[0]` through `x[4]` are defined. Somewhere in the program the term `x[n]` appears. Find out what happens if at some point, `n` inadvertently becomes 5, and the system tries to evaluate the term `x[n]`.

(b) Suppose we have this loop in a program:

```
for (n = 0;  n < 6;  n++)
    x[n] = x[n] + 1;
```

In other words, it is clear from the outset that `x[5]` will occur. Does the compiler spot this, or must the system wait until the program runs?

(c) Suppose `x[5]` appears explicitly. What happens?

EXPERIMENT 6-7

(a) Use `#define` to define an integer constant `N` equal to `10`. See if an array variable can be declared like this: `int x[N];`.

(b) Given a declaration of the form `int x[?]`. Determine how large the `?` can be. (It depends on your machine.)

(c) Suppose we have an integer *variable*, say, n, to which we will assign a value when the program runs. Can one declare an array as in part (a), using n? What does this say about when the size of an array must be known?

6.2.3 Sorting: An Application Using Arrays

In general, *sorting* means putting in order. It is often desirable to sort a list of values, for example, from the smallest to the largest. The reason is simple: It is easier to find a particular value from a sorted list than from an unsorted one.

There are many ways to sort a list. If we didn't know any better, we might try something like this: Find the smallest value on the list, cross it off, then write it on a new list. Now look over what remains of the original list. Pick out the smallest value, cross it off the list, and write it on the new list following the previous entry. Do this over and over until all the values in the original list have been crossed off. The result: a new list that is sorted.

The foregoing is a pretty crude approach. If the list were large, this routine would waste quite a bit of time with unnecessary busywork. It would also waste space, since two lists are required. Can we improve on this? After a course in data structures, the answer will be "Quite a bit!". For now, we will have to settle for a more modest "Somewhat."

The sort we have chosen to illustrate is called the *selection sort*. It is similar to the above, except that we don't need a new list. Hence, it is "somewhat" of an improvement over what was described above (it takes less space). The selection sort works like this (refer to Figure 6.5): When the smallest value of list `L` is found, it is swapped with the first item on the existing list rather than placed on another list. This means that `L[0]`, now the smallest element, is in its proper place, and needs no further consideration. The "current list," which is what we shall call the remaining elements, is then examined and *its* smallest value is swapped with the first item. Now `L[0]` and `L[1]` are in their proper places, and the current list is considered to begin with `L[2]`. The foregoing process is repeated until all elements of the original list have been put in their proper places.

Summary of Program 6.2

Strategy: The heart of Program 6.2 is a `for` loop whose counter (`count`) keeps track of the beginning of the current list. This loop calls two functions: `examine`, which returns the index of the smallest element of the current list, and `swap`, which swaps the smallest element of the list with the first one. Note that the `for` loop stops

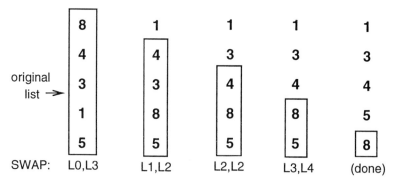

Figure 6.5   Selection Sort.

when `count` reaches the next to last array index, since the last remaining element will automatically be in its proper place if all the rest of them are.

The function `examine` simply loops through all the elements on the current list, and keeps track of which is the smallest. This was the subject of an example in Section 6.1. The function `swap` is even simpler, and was the subject of Exercise (2-6) from Chapter 2.

Exercises

(6-1) For each declaration, determine if it is *always* legal, *sometimes* legal, or *never* legal. Explain your answers.

```
(a) float x[5.0];
(b) int x[n];
(c) int x[x];
(d) int x[five];
(e) char x[ ];
(f) char [ ] = {a,b,c,d,e};
(g) char [ ] = {'Q','U','I','T'};
(h) char [7] = {'Q','U','I','C','K','L','Y'};
```

(6-2) What is the output of this program?

```
void main( )
  {
    int od[10], ev[10], k[10];
    int n;

    for (n = 0;  n < 10;  n++)
      {
        ev[n] = 2*n;
        od[n] = 1;
      }
```

```
    for (n = 0;  n < 10;  n++)
        scanf("%d", &k[n]);

    for (n = 0;  n < 10;  n++)
        if (k[n] % 2 == 0)
            ev[n] = k[n];
        else od[9 - n] = k[n];

    for (n = 0;  n < 10;  n++)
        printf("%d %d \n", ev[n], od[n]);
}
```

INPUT = 6 3 12 14 9 6 7 5 3 10

(6-3) What is the output of this program?

```
    int out(int);

    void main( )
      {
        int k[10];
        int n;

        for (n = 0;  n < 10;  n++)
            scanf("%d", &k[n]);
        for (n = 0;  n < 10;  n++)
            if( (out(k[n]) == 1)
               k[k[n]] = k[n];
        for (n = 0;  n < 10;  n++)
            printf("%d \n",k[n]);
      }

     int  out(int x)
      {
        int j;

        if ((x % 2) == 1)
            j = 1;
        else j = 0;
        return (j);
      }
```

INPUT = 6 3 12 14 9 6 7 5 3 10

(6-4) What is the output of this program?

```
    void main( )
      {
        int k[10];
        int n;

        for (n = 0;  n < 10;  n++)
            scanf("%d", &k[n]);
```

```
for (n = 0;  n < 10;  n++)
   if (k[n] % 2 > 0)
      k[n/2] = k[n];
for (n = 0;  n < 10;  n++)
   printf("%d \n", k[n]);
}
```

INPUT = 6 3 12 14 9 6 7 5 3 10

(6-5) Suppose **x** and **y** are equal sized arrays of the same type. Why is the expression **x == y** legal, while the expression **x = y** is not?

(6-6) Is it incorrect, or merely unnecessary, to put the ampersand in front of an array name when it is passed as a parameter to a function?

(6-7) What code is needed to calculate the sum of all the elements of an array?

(6-8) What code is needed to calculate the *product* of all the elements of an array?

(6-9) At the outset of this section, we used the batting averages of ballplayers as an example of a quantity that could be represented by a one-dimensional array. How would such an array have to be indexed?

6.3

TWO-DIMENSIONAL ARRAYS

A *two-dimensional array* is the structure we use to represent a quantity that depends on two discrete variables. Such data can be pictured as a table (Figure 6.6), which shows the number of home runs hit by eight different teams in eight different games. Each combination of games and home runs is an element of a two-dimensional array that corresponds to the table. Some examples of other quantities that can be represented by two-dimensional arrays are listed below.

(a) The mean temperatures of each day *of each month*. The temperature depends on the month and the day.

(b) The batting averages of each player *on each team* in the major leagues. The batting average depends on the team and the player.

(c) The seating capacity of each room *of every building* on campus. The seating capacity depends on the building and the room.

(d) A table of coefficients for calculating insurance on our used car dealer's stock. Each coefficient depends on the type of vehicle and the rate class. (These are the numbers such as **24.5, 26.1,** etc. used to calculate costs in Programs 4.2 and 6.1.)

Figure 6.6 A table showing the number of home runs hit by eight different teams in eight different games.

	team 1	team 2	team 3	team 4	team 5	team 6	team 7	team 8
game 1	2	1	3	0	0	1	4	3
game 2	0	2	1	1	2	1	4	2
game 3	2	1	1	0	3	2	(1)	1
game 4	1	2	1	1	1	4	2	0
game 5	3	3	1	2	1	3	3	2
game 6	2	1	2	2	0	0	0	2
game 7	1	1	2	1	3	4	2	5
game 8	1	1	4	2	2	0	1	3

Program 6.3 is similar to Program 6.1, but rewritten to illustrate the use of a two-dimensional array. In particular, we have put all the coefficients alluded to in (d), above, in a two-dimensional array called `cf`. We have made this variable global to illustrate the use of a global variable.

The general ideas about one-dimensional arrays carry over to two dimensions. However, there are important differences.

(a) If we picture the array as a table, then each element is in a unique combination of row and column. Two indices are needed to specify an element: one to identify the row (*row index*), followed by one to identify the column (*column index*). If the entire array is denoted by `tab`, an individual element in the `i`-th row and `j`-th column is denoted by `tab[i-1][j-1]`. In Figure 6.6, for example, the circled element has the indices `[2][6]`. Lines `[2][4]` of Program 6.3 give many instances of elements of the array `cf` being accessed.

(b) The declaration must have a pair of square brackets for the column dimension, followed by a pair of square brackets for the row dimension. This is illustrated in line `[1]` of Program 6.3. Note that the column dimension is numerically equal to the number of elements in a row. The row dimension is numerically equal to the number of elements in a column.

(c) The size of the array—the total number of elements—is the product of the two dimensions: the number of rows times the number of columns.

(d) When specifying a two-dimensional array as a formal parameter, it is necessary to specify the second dimension, though not the first. For example, `tempera-`

`ture[][30]` is legal as a formal parameter; `temperature[][]`, however, is not. We will explain why in the next section.

(e) A two-dimensional array can also be viewed as a one-dimensional array whose elements are themselves one-dimensional arrays.

Examples: **Declarations for Two-Dimensional Array**

Here are possible array declarations for the examples above:

```
float      temperature[12][31];
int        batter[16][25];
int        roomsize[18][40];
float      cf[3][3];
```

Example: **Declaration with Initialization**

Line `[1]` of Program 6.3 also illustrates the initialization of a two-dimensional array in the declaration:

```
float  cf[3][3] = { {22.3, 22.3, 26.1},
                    {24.5, 22.3, 24.5},
                    {22.3, 24.5, 22.7} };
```

Note that each row is surrounded by a pair of braces, and the entire set of rows (two, in this case) is surrounded by still another pair of braces.

The row dimension can be left out when initializing in the declaration. However, the column dimension *cannot* be left out. This, too, is explained in the next section. In general, the declaration for an array with **m** rows and **n** columns is:

```
<type name>    <var name>[m][n] = {{value list 1},...{value list m}};
```

We can leave out the **m**, or we can leave out everything to the right of `[n]` except the semicolon. We cannot leave out both of these, however.

6.3.1 Two-Dimensional Array Arithmetic

Consider an array declared as `int x[5][3]`. We will assume that each integer occupies four bytes. The array is stored in memory (Figure 6.7) as a sequence of **5** contiguous blocks of memory, each containing the elements of a single row. Thus, there are **5** blocks each with **3** elements. As in the one dimensional case, a key issue is calculating the address of an arbitrary element, say, `x[2][1]`. Recall that this boils down to finding the number of elements from the beginning of the array to `x[2][1]`. The **2** tells us that `x[2][1]` is at least two complete rows from the beginning of the array. This is **2 * 3** elements, since there are three elements per row. Expressed in bytes, we get **4 * 2 * 3** bytes. The **1** tells us that we are one element beyond the last of the two rows. This is **4 * 1** bytes. With this information, we can now calculate the address of element `x[2][1]`:

```
address of x[2][1] = beginning address of array + 4 * (2 * 3 + 1)
```

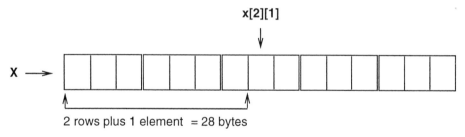

2 rows plus 1 element = 28 bytes

Figure 6.7   Finding element x[2][1] in an array of five rows of three elements each}.

We can generalize the above to find the address of element `x[i][j]` in an arbitrary array `x[m][n]` whose elements occupy `k` bytes per element. By making these substitutions:

$$5 \to m; \; 4 \to k; \; 3 \to n; \; 2 \to i; \; 1 \to j$$

we have that

```
address of x[i][j] = starting address  +  k * (i * n + j)
```

As in the one-dimensional case, the declaration carries with it the number of bytes per element (`k`), `i` and `j` are specified in the element identifier, and the array name is essentially the starting address. The additional information required here—`n`—is the *number of elements per row*. This explains why a formal parameter that is a two-dimensional array must have the column dimension specified: The column dimension is the number of elements per row.

Finally, there is the issue of what the identifier `x` itself means. We can guess that `x` is a constant pointer to the beginning of the array, just as in the one-dimensional case. Let us perform Experiment 6-8, which will hopefully shed more light on this.

EXPERIMENT 6-8:

Consider an array with this declaration:

```
int    x[3][3] = { {1, 2, 3}, {10, 20, 30}, {100, 200, 300}};
```

First print out the locations of `x[0][0]` and `x[1][0]`. Then execute these lines:

```
printf("%u %u \n", x, *x);
printf("%u %u \n", x+1, *x + 1);
printf("%u %u \n", x[0], *x[0]);
```

Note the output of each quantity.

To understand this experiment, it is important to remember that the two-dimensional array `x` is basically a one-dimensional array whose elements are themselves one dimensional arrays. For the one-dimensional array `A`, we know these two things:

1. An array name A is a pointer to the first element of the array.

2. The quantity *A is the name of the first element.

From (1), we conclude that the quantity **x** must be a pointer to the first element of a one-dimensional array of one-dimensional arrays. That is, **x** must point to the first row of the two-dimensional array. Therefore, from (2), the quantity *x must be the name of the first row itself. But the name of the first row is just a pointer to the first element of the row, since the row is a one-dimensional array. Hence, both **x** and *x are pointers. Furthermore, they both point to the same place, as evidenced by the output of the first line of the code.

The second line of output shows us that although **x** and *x point to the same place, they are not the same type of pointer! If they were, then adding **1** to each pointer value would give the same value. Clearly this is not the case. The quantity **x** + **1** points to the next *row*, while *x + **1** points to the next *element*. This is consistent with the foregoing discussion. The identifier **x** is the name of the two-dimensional array, and therefore points to its first element, which is a whole row. The quantity *x is the name of a row, and therefore points to the row's first element, which is an individual integer.

The third line shows that the notation **x[n]** is meaningful even for a two-dimensional array. Since *x[0] is the first element of the first row, **x[0]** must be a pointer to that element. In other words, **x[0]** is the name of the first row of the two-dimensional array. More generally, **x[n]** is the name of row **n** of the array **x**.

Summary of Program 6.3

Strategy: Identical to that of Program 6.1, except that a global two-dimensional array containing all the insurance rate multipliers for the three types of vehicles is used for the calculations.

Style: No new style points in this program.

Exercises

(6-10) What is the size of the following arrays?

```
float x[4][10];
char ch[3][3];
float x[4][4][6];
```

(6-11) What is the output from this program?

```
void main( )
{
  int   a,b;
  int   tab[4][4];
```

```
        for (a = 0;  a < 4;  a++)
          for (b = 0;  b < 4;  b++)
             scanf("%d", &tab[a][b]);
        for (b = 0;  b < 4;  b++)
          for (a = 0;  a < 4;  a++)
             printf("%d \n", tab[a][b]);
     }
```

INPUT: 1 7 4 2 5 9 12 8 20 30 2 7 6 4 11 6

(6-12) What is the output from this program?

```
     void main( )
      {
        int  a,b;
        int  tab[4][4];

        for (a = 0;  a < 4;  a++)
          for (b = 0;  b < 4;  b++)
             scanf("%d", &tab[a][b]);
        for (a = 0;  a < 4;  a++)
          for (b = 0;  b < 4;  b++)
             printf("%d \n", tab[3-a][b]);
     }
```

INPUT: 1 7 4 2 5 9 12 8 20 30 2 7 6 4 11 6

(6-13) What is the output from this program?

```
     void main( )
      {
        int  a,b;
        int  tab[4][4];

        for (a = 0;  a < 4;  a++)
          for (b = 0;  b < 4;  b++)
             scanf("%d", &tab[a][b]);
        for (a = 0;  a < 4;  a++)
          for (b = 0;  b < 4;  b++)
             if( (tab[a][b] % 2) != (tab[b][a] % 2) )
                tab[a][b] = 0;
        for (a = 0;  a < 4;  a++)
          for (b = 0;  b < 4;  b++)
             printf("%d \n", tab[a][b]);
     }
```

INPUT: 1 7 4 2 5 9 12 8 20 30 2 7 6 4 11 6

(6-14) What is the output from this program?

```
     void main( )
      {
        int  a,b;
        int  tab[4][4];
```

```
for (a = 0;  a < 4;  a++)
    for (b = 0;  b < 4;  b++)
        scanf("%d", &tab[a][b]);
for (a = 0;  a < 4;  a++)
    for (b = 0;  b < 4;  b++)
        if (tab[a][b] % 2 == 0)
            tab[a][b] = 1;
for (a = 0;  a < 4;  a++)
    for (b = 0;  b < 4;  b++)
        printf("%d \n", tab[3-a][3-b]);
}
```

INPUT: 1 7 4 2 5 9 12 8 20 30 2 7 6 4 11 6

(6-15) What code would be necessary if we wished to read the values of cf in Program 6.3 from the keyboard?

(6-16) What code will find the sum of the third column of cf in Program 6.3?

(6-17) Repeat the above, only write the code that finds the sum of the third row.

(6-18) Suppose we have an array with n rows and m columns. What is the code for the sum of the k-th row? The k-th column?

(6-19) What is the code that sums the elements on the main diagonal of a square array (one where the number of rows equals the number of columns)?

(6-20) Consider an array x. Does x+n represent the same number of bytes beyond the beginning of the array as x[0]+n?

6.4

STRINGS

Generally speaking, a *string* is a sequence of characters concatenated one after the other. In *C*, there are two kinds of strings that are of special interest to us: the *string constant*, and the *string variable*. A string constant is any string that is enclosed in a pair of double quotes. For example, the quantities "house" and "mjr78" are string constants, while house and mjr78 are not. A string variable is a variable whose possible values are string constants.

C has string variables, but the data type name is not "string," or anything similar. Instead, *C* represents strings as arrays of characters.

Examples: **Declaration for Strings**

```
char     strg[9];
char     message[15];
char     single_character[2];
```

Consider the first of the above declarations. Since this is an array declaration, `strg` must be a constant pointer that points to the first character of the array. Although `strg` is declared as a nine-character array, `strg[8]` is not necessarily its last character. Instead, the special character `\0`, called the *null character*, marks the end of the string, and this can occur before `strg[8]`. We can therefore say, in general, that a string declared to be an `n`-character array has a maximum of `n-1` characters.

The third declaration above—`char single_character[2]`—is a string of one character. It should not be confused with a character variable. From the above discussion, we can see that a string of one character actually has two characters, the second one being the null character.

Almost all manipulations with strings require special built in *string handling* functions. In this section, the only manipulations we will be interested in are assignment, input, and output. For these, we need to introduce only one string handling function, which we will do shortly. Note that when using string handling functions, it is necessary to include the header file `string.h`.

String Assignment: Assigning values to strings is a bit unusual. One approach is to initialize a string in the declaration. Here are two such declarations:

```
char     strg[9] = { 'm', 'e', 'l', 'o', 'n', '\0' };
char     strg[9] = "melon";
```

The first declaration is nothing more than the usual list of values that is part of an array declaration with initialization. Note that the null character must be inserted explicitly. The second declaration—assigning a value to the entire array at once, rather than listing the individual elements—is unique to strings. Here the null character is put in automatically.

EXPERIMENT 6-9

Using the assignment operator, try to assign the value `melon` to a string. What happens?

To overcome the difficulty pinpointed by this experiment, we will use a string handling function that at first glance does not appear to have anything to do with assignment. This is the `strcpy` function, which copies one string to another. For example,

```
strcpy(fruit, melon);
```

replaces the current value of `fruit` with the five characters of `melon`. The previous value of `fruit` is wiped out. In general,

```
strcpy(<target string>, <source string>);
```

replaces `<target string>` with a copy of `<source string>`.[2] For all intents and purposes, this function effectively "assigns" the value of the source string to the target string.

String Input: We can read a value of a string using `scanf`. This works in the usual way, except that we must use the format specifier appropriate for strings: `%s`. To assign the value `melon` to the string `strg` using the `scanf` statement, we write:

```
scanf("%s", strg);
```

and type the word *melon* when the system pauses for input. Note that there is no ampersand before the identifier `strg`, since it is already an address.

String Output: Using the format specifier `%s`, we can output a string using `printf`:

```
printf("%s \n", strg);
```

Note that the `%s` format specifier requires a pointer in the corresponding place in the variable list. As the next experiment shows, the pointer is assumed to point to a sequence of characters terminated by the null character.

EXPERIMENT 6-10

Consider these declarations:

```
float     z = 555555555.5;
float     *q;
char      x[] = "hello";
char      *p;
```

Run a program that points `p` to the string `x`, and `q` to the number `z`, then prints out `p` and `q` using the string format specifier. Explain the output.

Arrays of Pointers

We will now look at something that, on the surface, is quite simple: a one-dimensional array of pointers to characters. An example of such an array is the following:

```
char      *cars[3];
```

---

2 The source string can be either a string constant or a string variable. The target must be a variable!

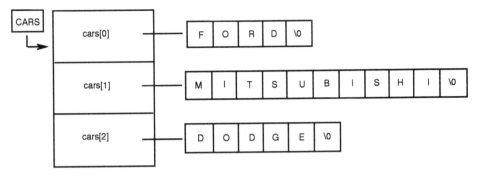

Figure 6.8   An array of strings.

Since this is an array of three pointers (i.e., addresses), one might think it is impossible to initialize it in the declaration. After all, we don't know actual addresses, so how can we make a list of their values? As it happens, we initialize this array following the usual rules:

```
char    *cars[3] = {"FORD", "MITSUBISHI", "DODGE"};
```

This is a list of three string constants. Since these are really just pointers, the above declaration is simply a list of three constants that point to arrays of characters, precisely the data type of the array elements. Figure 6.8 illustrates the complete structure. `cars` is a constant pointer to the first element of an array. This array consists of three addresses: `cars[0]`, `cars[1]`, and `cars[2]`. Note that the addresses need not be addresses of equal-length strings. This is an advantage of storing these strings as an array of pointers.

In the following experiment, we will look at the array described above. It is a good test of one's understanding of the relation between arrays and pointers.

EXPERIMENT 6-11

Using the declarations above, run a program that contains the following statements. Try to predict the outcome of the first three before you run the program.

```
printf("%s \n", cars[1]);
printf("%c \n", cars[1][2]);
printf("%c \n", *cars[1]);
printf("%u \n", cars);
printf("%u %u %u \n", cars[0], cars[1], cars[2]);
```

Use the last result to determine if your computer stores the three strings one after the other.

Exercises

(6-21) Instead of storing the three strings discussed above in a one-dimensional array of pointers, store them in a two-dimensional array of characters. Compare the space required for both methods.

(6-22) A programmer wishes to write a program to simulate various card games. In it, she needs four strings: `SPADES`, `HEARTS`, `CLUBS`, and `DIAMONDS`. She declares a variable `card` as an array of pointers to characters, and initializes the array with a list of the four string constants written in alphabetical order. Draw a schematic diagram of this structure. Identify the data type of each of the following quantities:

```
1 -  card[3]
2 - *card[3]
3 - *card
```

Programming Problems

(6-P1) Write a program that merges two one-dimensional arrays into a single array twice as large.

Program Input: Two one-dimensional arrays of ten integers each.

Program Output: A one-dimensional array of size twenty whose elements are drawn alternately from each of the two input arrays.

(6-P2) Write a program that determines whether or not a word is a palindrome (one that is the same when read either forwards or backwards).

Program Input: A word that is at most ten characters.

Program Output: `Palindrome.` or `Not palindrome.` depending on the input word.

(6-P3) Write a program that reads a list of integers, sorts them in ascending order, then finds the product of the largest two.

Program Input: A list of up to fifteen integers.

Program Output: Two statements:

```
The sorted list is ... (list values)
The product of the two largest values is ... (product)
```

(6-P4) Write a program that reads a list of integers, then determines for each one how many of the previous integers on the list divide evenly into it.

Program Input: A list of at most fifteen integers.

Program Output: Fifteen lines of output: the element number, followed by the number of preceding elements that evenly divide into it. For example, if the seventh element on the list can be evenly divided by the fourth and fifth elements, the output would be 7 2.

(6-P5) Write a function that finds the element closest in value to the first element in the first row of a two-dimensional array.

Function Input: A two-dimensional array of integers (ten rows and ten columns).

Function Output: A 0 to indicate that the task was completed. The row and column indices of the element closest in value to element [0,0] should be output through two parameters.

(6-P6) Write a function that initializes a two-dimensional array so that an element is 1 if the sum of the row and column indices is odd, and -1 if the sum is even.

Function Input: An uninitialized two-dimensional array of integers (ten rows and ten columns).

Function Output: A 0 to indicate that the task was completed. The initialization should take place through the parameters of the function.

(6-P7) Write a program that multiplies a four-by-four matrix **a** by another four-by-four matrix **b**. The product is a four-by-four matrix whose elements are defined as follows:

$$(ab)_{i,j} = \sum_{k=1}^{4} a_{i,k} b_{k,j}$$

Program Input: Thirty-two integers representing two four-by-four arrays of integers.

Program Output: A printout of the sixteen integers that comprise the product of the two input matrices.

(6-P8) Write a program that prints graphically all positions to which a bishop can move from its given position on a chessboard.

Program Input: The row and column indices denoting the current position of a bishop.

Program Output: An eight-by-eight grid consisting of mostly asterisks, a single B representing the current position of the bishop, and the letter M in each place to which the bishop can legally move.

(6-P9) Repeat the above problem for a queen.

(6-P10) Write a program that searches a two-dimensional array for the presence of a three-letter word. The word can be in a row, a column, or a diagonal, in either direction.

Program Input: A two-dimensional array of characters, six rows and six columns.

Program Output: The row and column indices of the elements where the matching word is stored. If no match is found, the program should indicate this.

(6-P11) Write a program to simulate rolling a single die fifty times. (You will need the `rand` and `srand` functions for this.)

User Input: An integer **n**, which is a request for the result of the nth roll. Integers less than 1 and greater than 50 must be rejected, then input again.

Program Output: The result of the **n**-th roll.

(6-P12) Modify Program Problem (6-P11) so that it simulates fifty rolls of `three` dice.

User Input: Two integers—m and n—that constitute a request for the value of the nth roll of the mth die.

Program Output: The result of the **n**-th roll of the **m**-th die.

(6-P13) Consider the problem of simulating the roll of three dice. Write a program that calculates the probability of getting a particular sum of the three dice. (Question: How many rolls do you think you need to simulate?)

User Input: None.

Program Output: A simple chart showing sum versus probability for all possible sums.

PROGRAMS FOR CHAPTER SIX

Program 6.1: Using a One-Dimensional Array

```
       #include<stdio.h>

[1]    float calculate_rate_1(int[]);
[2]    float calculate_rate_2(int[]);
[3]    float calculate_rate_3(int[]);

       main()
        {
          int     n, rate_class;
[4]       int     vehicle[3];                /* vehicle[0] is bikes
                                                 vehicle[1] is cars,
                                                 vehicle[2] is trucks */

          printf("Enter the number of bikes, then cars, then
                  trucks,\n");
          printf("then rate class [1, 2, or 3]. \n");

[5]       for (n = 0; n < 3; n++)
              scanf("%d", &vehicle[n]);
          scanf("%d", &rate_class);

          switch (rate_class)
            {
[6]           case 1: printf("Total cost is %f dollars \n",
                          calculate_rate_1(vehicle));
                      break;
              case 2: printf("Total cost is %f dollars \n",
                          calculate_rate_2(vehicle));
                      break;
              case 3: printf("Total cost is %f dollars \n",
                          calculate_rate_3(vehicle));
            }
        }

  /* This function calculates the cost of insurance for all vehichles
     based on rate class 1.

     Input: array of integers.  Output: insurance cost (float).    */

[7] float calculate_rate_1(int v[])
      {
        float rate;
        rate = 22.3*v[0] + 22.3*v[1] + 26.1*v[2];
        return(rate);
      }
```

```
/* This function calculates the cost of insurance for all vehichles
      based on rate class 2.

      Input: array of integers.  Output: insurance cost (float).    */

   float calculate_rate_2(int v[])
     {
       float rate;
       rate = 24.5*v[0] + 22.3*v[1] + 24.5*v[2];
       return(rate);
     }

/* This function calculates the cost of insurance for all vehichles
      based on rate class 3.
      Input: array of integers.  Output: insurance cost (float).    */

   float calculate_rate_3(int v[])
     {
       float rate;
       rate = 22.3*v[0] + 24.5*v[1] + 22.3*v[2];
       return(rate);
     }
```

Program 6.2: A Sorting Routine

```
#include<stdio.h>

int    examine(int, int, int[]);

void   swap(int *, int *);

main()
{
  int  count,                    /* index of beginning of each list */
       smallest,       /* index of smallest value for each list */
       listsize = 5;            /* number of items on the list*/

  int    list[] = { 4, 8, 3, 1, 5 };

  /* This is essentially the program.  The function "examine"
     returns the index of the element of the current list with
     the smallest value; the function "swap" exchanges the first
     element on the current list with the element whose index is
     smallest.  */

  for(count = 0; count < listsize - 1; count++)
    {
        smallest = examine(count, listsize - 1, list);
        swap(&list[smallest], &list[count]);
    }

   for (count = 0; count < listsize; count++)
      printf("%d \n", list[count]);
}
```

```
int  examine(int n, int  size, int  z[])
{
  int    temp, m;
  temp = n;
  /* "temp" keeps track of the index of the element
      with the smallest value.   */

  for (m = n; m <= size; m++)
     if (z[m] < z[temp])
          temp = m;
  return(temp);
}

void swap(int *a, int *b)
{
  int    temp;
   temp = *a;
  *a = *b;
  *b = temp;
 }
```

Program 6.3: Using a Two-Dimensional Array

```
      #include<stdio.h>
      float calculate_rate_1(int[]);
      float calculate_rate_2(int[]);
      float calculate_rate_3(int[]);

[1]   float  cf[3][3] = { {22.3, 22.3, 26.1}, {24.5, 22.3, 24.5},
                      {22.3, 24.5, 22.7} };

      main()
      {
        int    n, rate_class, vehicle[3];

        for (n = 0; n < 3; n++)
           scanf("%d", &vehicle[n]);

        scanf("%d", &rate_class);

        switch (rate_class)
          {
           case 1: printf("Total cost is %f dollars \n",
                    calculate_rate_1(vehicle));
                    break;
           case 2: printf("Total cost is %f dollars \n",
                    calculate_rate_2(vehicle));
                    break;
           case 3: printf("Total cost is %f dollars \n",
                    calculate_rate_3(vehicle));
          }
      }

   /* This function calculates the insurance cost for all vehicles
      based on rate class 1.
```

```
        Input: array of integers.   (array cf is global!)
        Output: total insurance cost (float).                    */

     float calculate_rate_1(int v[])
        {
        float r;
[2]     r = cf[0][0]*v[0] + cf[0][1]*v[1] + cf[0][2]*v[2];
        return(r);
        }
```

```
/* This function calculates the insurance cost for all vehicles
     based on rate class 2.

        Input: array of integers.   (array cf is global!)
        Output: total insurance cost (float).                    */

     float calculate_rate_2(int v[])
        {
        float r;
[3]     r = cf[1][0]*v[0] + cf[1][1]*v[1] + cf[1][2]*v[2];
        return(r);
        }
```

```
/* This function calculates the insurance cost for all vehicles
     based on rate class 3.

        Input: array of integers.   (array cf is global!)
        Output: total insurance cost (float).                    */

     float calculate_rate_3(int v[])
        {
        float r;
[4]     r = cf[2][0]*v[0] + cf[2][1]*v[1] + cf[2][2]*v[2];
        return(r);
        }
```

7 Structs and Linked Lists

Program for Chapter Seven

• Program 7.1: Structs and a linked list

While an array is an important and useful data structure, it is limited by the fact that for a given array, all elements must be the same data type. There are many occasions when it is convenient to group different data types as a single unit. Consider, for example, the needs of a car dealer who keeps records of each car in stock. Without a computer, the dealer might maintain some sort of paper form with a variety of *fields*, places on the form for information pertaining to one car: its brand, price, number of doors, etc. In the digital computer era, such records are kept on magnetic media. The *idea* is the same, though: grouping together related items of (possibly) differing data types. The *C* equivalent of a record is known as a *structure*.

In this chapter, we will use structures to develop a so-called *linked list*. This can be useful for our hypothetical car dealer. First of all, each element of the list will be a structure that contains important information about a given vehicle. Second, the size of the list can expand when the dealer gets a shipment of cars from the factory, thereby increasing the total stock, and shrink when one or more sales reduces the stock. This is what Program 7.1 illustrates. It will take most of this chapter for us to develop the foundation needed to understand this program. That is because we are introducing a number of new ideas, and because the concepts behind Program 7.1 are more sophisticated than those we have encountered up to now.

7.1

STRUCTS

Our discussion of structures will attempt to answer the same questions that we posed for arrays at the beginning of the preceding chapter. However, we shall begin somewhat differently from our treatment of arrays. Recall that the array variables we used were always defined in terms of existing data types: arrays of integers, arrays of characters, etc. Since a structure can be just about any combination of data types, we first need to define precisely what the particular combination is. That is, we need to be able to define a data type that is tailored to our own needs. Such a type is called a *user-defined data type*. Only after doing this can we declare variables of that new type.

7.1.1 Declaring the Struct Type

The new data type that we will define is known generically as the *struct* data type. An example of how to define this is given below. It is similar to, but not exactly the same as, the data type declared in line [1] of Program 7.1:

```
struct vehicle
    {
        char      name[15];
        char      ident[10];
        float     price;
        int       doors;
    };
```

The name of this particular data type is `struct vehicle`. Note that this type has two names: the keyword `struct`, followed by a name of our choosing. Between the right and left braces is a list of variable declarations. These describe the data that are being grouped together. In the above example, it is our intention to group the name, identification code, price, and number of doors for each vehicle. The identifiers `name[20]`, `ident[10]`, `price`, and `doors` are called the structure's *members*.[1] As we shall see, they are *not* the names of variables. Going back to the aforementioned paper record, we can say that a structure is analogous to a template for the record, while the members are analogous to the fields.

As illustrated by the first two lines, members of a structure need not be simple data types. As long as their data types are known to the compiler, they can be used. Indeed, a member can even be a structure. However, it cannot be a structure of the type currently being defined. For example, we could *not* have

```
struct vehicle
    {
        char          name[15];
        char          ident[10];
        float         price;
```

---

1 The structure in this program could have been set up with many more members. We've kept it simple so that we can concentrate on the basic ideas concerning structures.

```
     int          doors;
     struct vehicle  vcl;
};
```

because `vcl` has a data type whose definition is not yet fully known to the compiler. However, we *can* do this (as in line [1] of Program 7.1):

```
struct vehicle
{
    char          name[15];
    char          ident[10];
    float         price;
    int           doors;
    struct vehicle  *next;
};
```

since `next` is declared as a *pointer*, not `struct vehicle` itself.

The type name `struct vehicle` is somewhat clumsy. We can simplify it as illustrated in line [2] of Program 7.1:

```
typedef struct vehicle NODE;
```

The purpose of the keyword `typedef` is to give an alias to an existing typename. We simply use `typedef` followed by the old and new type names, respectively. Thus `struct vehicle` is now called `NODE`.

7.1.2 Struct Variables

Having defined a data type `NODE`, we can now declare variables of that type. This is done in the usual way, with the type name, followed by the variable name. For example, to declare `x` and `y` as variables of type `NODE`, we do this:

```
NODE        x, y;
```

Accessing Individual Components: Unlike an array, the components of a structure are not distinguished from one another by indices. To access an individual component, we have an unusual looking notation involving two identifiers and a dot. For example, the structure variable `x` has these four components: `x.name`, `x.ident`, `x.price`, and `x.doors`. These components are treated the way any variable is treated.

Examples: **Using Structure Member Names**

```
strcpy(x.name, "FORD");
printf("The ID number is %s \n", x.id);
x.price = 13075.95;
x.doors = 4;
```

In general, a component variable of a structure is denoted this way:

```
<struct variable name>.<member name>
```

Now we can see that a member name by itself is not a variable. It takes a combination of member name and structure variable name to denote the variable that represents a particular component of the structure.

As with other variables, we can initialize a structure variable in the declaration. We simply list, between a pair of braces, the desired values for each member.

Example: Initializing a Structure

We could have replaced the four assignment statements above with this declaration:

```
NODE    x = {"FORD", "274-4413", 13075.95, 4};
```

The various names associated with structures can be a source of confusion, so let's quickly review what we have learned. Our example involves five variable names: `x`, which is the entire structure, and `x.name`, `x.ident`, `x.price`, and `x.doors`, which are the names of the component variables. `NODE` is a type name. The identifiers `name`, `ident`, `price`, and `doors` are neither type names nor variable names. Therefore, they never appear by themselves in expressions. They can appear alone only in the original `struct` declaration.

Passing Struct as Parameters

An entire structure can be passed as a parameter using either pass by value or by reference.[2] The following code, which passes a structure of type `NODE` to a function called `test`, illustrates pass by value:

```
        ...
main()
  {
        NODE   z = {"FORD", "2234-25-22", 15095, 4};
        ...
        test(z);
  }

void test(NODE st)
  {
     printf("%s  %s  %f %d \n", st.name, st.ident, st.price,
          st.doors);
  }
```

The rules are precisely those described in our discussion of parameter passing. When `z` is passed to `test`, the variables `z.name`, `z.ident`, `z.price`, and `z.doors` are copied to temporary locations `st.name`, `st.ident`, `st.price`, and `st.doors`, respectively. After the function finishes executing, these locations become undefined.

With three changes to the above code, we can easily illustrate pass by reference. First, the function header is changed to look like this:

```
     void   test(NODE *st);
```

---

2 Of course, the individual components can also be passed following the rules we have already discussed.

Second, the function call is changed to look like this:

```
test(&z);
```

The third change involves a different way of denoting the components of a structure when a pointer to the structure is involved. In the function `test`, the parameter `st` is a pointer to a structure of type **NODE**. Hence, the structure itself is `*st`. The components of `*st` can therefore be written as:

```
(*st).name
(*st).ident
(*st).price
(*st).doors
```

The parentheses are needed because the dot has a higher precedence than the dereferencing operator. This notation is rather clumsy, so we use something different: the *struct pointer operator ->*. Then the components can be written:

```
st->name
st->ident
st->price
st->doors
```

The third change is therefore a change to the `printf` statement in `test`:

```
printf("%s %s %f %d \n", st->name, st->ident, st->price, st->doors);
```

As is always the case with pass by reference, the locations of the actual parameters—`z->name`, `z->ident`, `z->price`, and `z->doors`—are the ones used by the function. No temporary structure is created.

7.2

DYNAMIC MEMORY ALLOCATION

We have seen how the allocation of space for a variable is taken care of in a declaration statement. The case of a pointer declaration is a bit unusual, though. Consider, for example, a declaration such as `int *p;`. Here, the integer `*p` is implicitly declared along with `p` itself, although no space is actually allocated for `*p`. In fact, `*p` is meaningless until `p` is pointed to an integer, say, `q`. At that point, `*p` denotes the space occupied by `q`.

It is possible to allocate space explicitly for `*p`. The way to do this is especially interesting because the allocation takes place *while the program is executing*. This idea, called *dynamic memory allocation*, is the basis of Program 7.1. To allocate memory while a program executes, we will need a new unary operator called the *cast* operator, along with two built-in C functions:

- **sizeof:** This function takes a data type name as input, and returns the number of bytes needed to store a variable of that type.

- **malloc:** This takes as input a specified number of bytes, allocates that many bytes of actual memory, and returns a pointer (of type **void**) to the beginning of the space allocated.

The basic idea is to compute the number of bytes needed for a particular variable, then ask `malloc`[3] to allocate that number of bytes. `malloc` returns a `void` pointer because it is told only how many bytes to allocate, not what type of space is being allocated. It is our job to change this pointer from type `void` to the appropriate type. We do this using a unary operator called the *cast operator*. This operator simply forces a conversion from one type to another. The cast operator consists of the desired type name enclosed in a pair of parentheses.

Example: **Cast Operation**

```
int     y;
float   x;
   ...
y = (int)x;
```

Here, the statement `y = (int)x` turns the floating point number `x` into an integer, then assigns the result to `y`. The contents of `x` are unchanged. Presumably we are careful in using this operation; casting `3.0` to `3` is fine, but casting `3.2` to `3` might not be.

Example: **Using `sizeof` and `malloc`**

In Program 7.1, line `[3]` demonstrates both the `sizeof` and `malloc` functions, along with the cast operation.

```
start = (NODE *)malloc(sizeof(NODE));
```

The function `sizeof` returns the number of bytes of memory required by a structure of type `NODE`. This is used as input to the function `malloc`, which allocates the required memory and returns a pointer to it. Since the latter is a pointer of type `void`, it needs to be cast as a pointer to type `NODE`. Hence the `(NODE *)` operation. Finally, the pointer is assigned to `start`.

EXPERIMENT 7-1

(a) Consider a program with the declaration `int *p` and these statements:

```
p = (int *)malloc(sizeof(int));
*p = 5;
p = (int *)malloc(sizeof(int));
*p = 8;
printf("%d \n, *p);
```

What does this result imply about the integer originally pointed to by `p` after the second invocation of `malloc`?

---

3 It is advisable to include the header file `stdlib.h` in programs that require `malloc`.

(b) Given the freedom to modify this program in any way, except by adding another `printf` statement, is there a way to write out the contents of the two locations? Would this be a good way to deal with, say, fifty invocations of `malloc`?

EXPERIMENT 7-2

(a) Assuming `p` and `q` point to integers, run the following program:

```
p = (int *)malloc(sizeof(int));
q = (int *)malloc(sizeof(int));
*p = 7;
*q = 10;
printf("%d \n", *p);
printf("%d \n", *q);
p = q;
printf("%d \n", *p);
printf("%d \n", *q);
*p = 7;
printf("%d \n", *p);
printf("%d \n", *q);
```

Note what gets written out each time.

(b) Run the same program except replace `p = q` by `*p = *q`. Note what gets written out. Carefully explain the different effect of these two assignment statements. (Diagrams are helpful here.)

7.2.1 Deallocation of Memory

One of the behind-the-scenes tasks of a computer is to keep internal lists indicating which memory locations have been allocated, and which are free (still available). If memory that was allocated by a call to `malloc` is no longer needed, it should be taken off the list of allocated memory, and put back on the list of free memory. This is easy to do:

```
free(p);
```

Here, `p` points to the location in question. That location is taken off the allocated list and put on the free list. Note that in order to free a location, something must point to it.

EXPERIMENT 7-3

Consider these statements (assume `int *p`):

```
p = (int *)malloc(sizeof(int));
*p = 5;
printf("%d \n", *p);
free(p);
printf("%d \n", *p);
```

Compile the above and run the program. Is the value of *p erased by the free function? What do we mean when we say that free "frees" the space allocated to *p?

Exercises

(7-1) Is there a shorthand way (such as an array variable in a loop) to access all the members of a struct variable?

(7-2) Is there any difference in the amount of space reserved by these calls:

```
(int *)malloc(sizeof(int *));
(float *)malloc(sizeof(float *));
        malloc(sizeof(void *));
```

Explain.

(7-3) Is there anything wrong with the following code?

```
int   *p;
*p = 10;
```

(7-4) For each of the following four exercises, draw a schematic diagram of the memory after each statement executes. Label the figure with variable names and contents of locations. If the value is unknown, use a ? as the contents of that location.

```
(a)    int   *p;
       int   num = 5;

       p = (int *)malloc(sizeof(int));
       *p = num;

(b)    int   *p;
       int   num = 5;

       p = (int *)malloc(sizeof(int));
       *p = num;
       free(p);

(c)    int   *p;
       int   num = 5;

       p = (int *)malloc(sizeof(int));
       p = (int *)malloc(sizeof(int));
       p = &num;

(d)    int   *p, *q;
       int   num = 5;
```

```
p = (int *)malloc(sizeof(int));
*p = num;
q = p;
p = &num;
free(q);
free(p);
```

7.3

LINKED LISTS

We begin our discussion of linked lists with a diagram, Figure 7.1. Each box in this diagram represents a single element of the list, called a *node*. A node may have many components; one of them *must* be a pointer to a variable whose type is precisely that of a node. The key to the linked list is that the pointer of one node points to the next node on the list. To indicate that the last node is indeed the last node, we set its pointer value to **NULL**, indicated by the diagonal line in the last box of Figure 7.1. This is the standard way to indicate the end of a linked list.

A node is implemented as a structure. For purposes of our discussion, we will use the **struct** defined below; we have encountered this already. An external pointer, which we call **start**—the only one not buried in the nodes themselves—points to the first node on the list. Note that without **start**, we would not be able to locate the list at all.

```
struct vehicle
    {
        char            name[15];
        char            ident[10];
        float           price;
        int             doors;
        struct vehicle  *next;
    };
typedef struct vehicle NODE;
```

We will answer four questions about linked lists:

How do we make an initial linked list?

How do we access the data in a given node?

How do we add a node anywhere on the list?

How do we delete any node from the list?

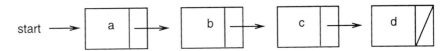

Figure 7.1   A linked list with four nodes.

Making the Initial List

To build a linked list, we first define three separate pointers to type NODE: start, p, and q. Then we execute the following sequence (see Figure 7.2):

1. Create a node using start = (NODE *)malloc(sizeof(NODE)).
2. Set another pointer, q, to point to this node.
3. Assign data (x in the diagram) to the nonpointer members of *q.
4. Create a new node using p = (NODE *)malloc(sizeof(NODE)).
5. Assign data (y in the diagram) to the nonpointer members of *p.
6. Point node *q to node *p.
7. Point q to *p.
8. Repeat steps (4) through (7) until no more nodes are needed.
9. Assign NULL to the pointer member of the last node.

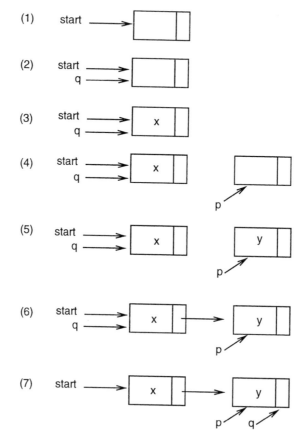

Figure 7.2   Creating a linked list. Numbers are keyed to the steps described in the text.

We are left with a linked list whose beginning is marked by `start`. Note that once `start` is put in place, it is *never* moved. Its sole function is to mark the beginning of the list. The actual *C* code to make the list is shown in `main()` of Program 7.1.

7.3.1 Accessing Individual Components

As with any structured data type, we need to know how to locate an arbitrary element. In the case of a linked list, the process might seem a bit clumsy. Suppose, for example, we want to get to node *d* of Figure 7.1. The address of *d* is found only in the preceding node, *c*. The address of *c* is found only in *b*, and so on. The only node whose address is not tucked away in another node is the first node; it is pointed to by `start`. Therefore, starting at the first node we find the address of the second. From the second we find the third, and so on until we are at node *d*. To access any node in a list, then, we must examine all the nodes that come before it!

A practical question arises: We start at the first node every time, but how do we know when to stop? The answer is simple: As we examine each node, we check to see if a particular component has a desired value. If it does, we simply leave the pointer where it is. If it does not, we move the pointer to the next node and examine it. The process is repeated until we find what we are looking for, or we have reached the end of the list.

EXPERIMENT 7-4

Create a linked list whose nodes are similar to type `NODE`. (Simplify the definition so that it has only one data member, `doors`. See to it that none of the nodes has a `doors` value of 5. Attempt to look for a node with a `doors` value of 5 using this code:

```
p = start;
while (p->doors != 5)
    p = p->next;
printf("%f \n", p->price);
```

What is the problem with this code?

Adding a Node to a Linked List

When our hypothetical dealer gets more vehicles, they can be added to the list in one of two ways: to the beginning of a list, or immediately following a specified node. Figure 7.3 illustrates the latter; we will add a node immediately following node **c**:

1. Move a pointer **q** from the beginning of the list until it points to the specified node.
2. Allocate memory for a new node and point another pointer **p** to the new node.
3. Point the new node ***p** to the same place where the specified node ***q** points.
4. Point the specified node ***q** to the new node.

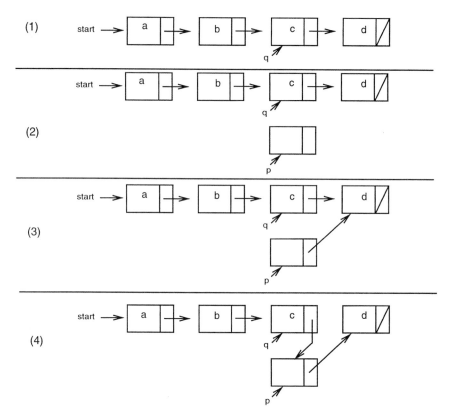

Figure 7.3   Adding a node to a linked list.

Once this is done, we can assign values to the various members of the new node `*p`. Programming Problem (7-P8) involves adding a node to a list.

Deleting a Node from a List

When the dealer sells a car, it should be removed from the list. To do this, we need to consider the node to be deleted, and the node that precedes it. The trick here is to recognize that when `p->next` points to a node, `p` points to the one preceding it. Figure 7.4 illustrates the procedure for deleting node `b`:

1. Move a pointer `q` from the beginning of the list so that it points to the node preceding the one to be deleted.
2. Set another pointer `p` to point to the node following `*q`.
3. Point the node `*q` to the node following `*p`. This leaves the node `*p` with nothing pointing to it.

Once this is done, we can deallocate the node `*p`. Programming Problem (7-P9) involves the deletion of a node from a linked list.

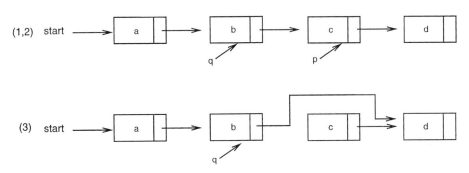

Figure 7.4   Deleting a node from a linked list. Steps are keyed to the steps described in the text.

Summary of Program 7.1

Strategy: First, the program defines the **struct** it will use for the nodes of the linked list. Then, using **malloc**, it allocates space for the first node, and points **start** to it (line [3]). The function **create_header** is used to assign values to the node that identifies the beginning of the list (line [4]). This is called a *header node*. Then a second pointer **p** is pointed to the list (line [5]). Now the **while** loop is entered. It points yet a third pointer **q** to point to where **p** currently points. Then space for a new node is allocated, and **p** is pointed to the new node (line [6]). Thus the loop essentially starts out with **p** pointing to the most recently created node, and **q** pointing to the one before it. From this point on, the loop does two things: (1) It assigns values to ***p**, the most recently created node. (2) It points the next to the last node, ***q**, to the last one, ***p** (line [7]). The loop repeats this process until the value of the sentinel is 0. Finally, the last node is marked with **NULL**.

Style:
- All three pointers are initialized before their first use.
- Comment calls attention to which variables are pointers.

Exercises

For this section of exercises, consider a five-element linked list whose nodes are of type **NODE** as defined above. Assume that the **doors** values are the integers **1** through **5** (we don't care about the other members), and that the list is pointed to by **start**.

(7-5) For both exercises below, draw the list after each of the statements has executed, showing where the pointer **q** points.

      (a)   `q = start->next;`

      (b)   `q = start->next->next;`

(7-6) What's wrong with this code?

```
p = start;
q = p;
while ( q->next != NULL )
        p = p->next;
```

(7-7) Set a pointer `p` to the first element on the list. Assume another pointer `q` points somewhere in the list, but you don't know where. Write the code to point `p` to the same element pointed to by `q`.

(7-8) Set a pointer `p` to the beginning of the list. Write the code needed to turn the list into a `circular` list (one where the "last" node is followed by the "first").

(7-9) Write the code necessary to delete the first node of a linked list. Then modify the code so that it deletes the last one.

(7-10) Modify the code for adding a node so that it adds a node to the beginning of a linked list.

(7-11) What is the consequence of reversing the order of the last two lines of the code that add a node?

Programming Problems

(7-P1) There is no complex number data type in C; a struct is an excellent way to define one:

```
typedef struct
    {   float   re;  /* real part */
        float   im;  /* imaginary part */
    } complex;
```

Write a function that adds two complex numbers. (The sum of two complex numbers is also complex. The real part of the sum is the sum of the real parts; the imaginary part of the sum is the sum of the imaginary parts.)

Function Input: Two variables of type `complex`.

Function Output: A variable of type `complex` that is the sum of the two inputs.

(7-P2) Consider an array of fifty of the following structs:

```
typedef struct
    { int     age;
      float   salary;
    } employee;
```

Write a function that creates an employee record at an arbitrary position in the above array.

Function Input: The array, an index into the array, a value of age, and a value of salary.

Function Output: None.

(7-P3) Using the struct defined in the previous problem, write a function that finds the employee earning the highest salary.

User Input: The array.

Program Output: The index of the employee earning the highest salary.

(7-P4) Write a program that initializes a chess board with all the pieces in the normal starting position. Note that a suitable struct must be defined before proceeding!

User Input: None.

Program Output: An eight-by-eight table showing how each square is occupied. Use an asterisk to denote an unoccupied position.

(7-P5) Write a program that initializes a chess board at an arbitrary point in the game.

User Input: Location and identity of each piece in the game.

Program Output: An eight-by-eight table showing how each square is occupied. Use an asterisk to denote an unoccupied position.

(7-P6) Write a program that, given an arbitrary chess game configuration, determines if any piece on one side threatens any of the opponent's pieces.

User Input: A game configuration, plus the identity of the threatening side.

Program Output: A list of all positions that are threatened.

(7-P7) Write a program that, given an arbitrary chess game configuration, determines if a given move is legal.

User Input: A game configuration, the original position of the moved piece, and the final position of the moved piece.

Program Output: `Legal move.` or `Illegal move.` as appropriate.

NOTE: The remaining exercises require some kind of manipulation of a linked list. It is therefore necessary to create such a list before answering each question. Keep the node simple; use just one data field, in addition to the pointer field.

(7-P8) Write a program that adds an element to a linked list.

User Input: Data for the node to be added, plus the identity of the node after which the new node is to be added.

Program Output: A printout of the data fields of all the nodes of the modified list.

(7-P9) Write a program that deletes an element from a linked list.

User Input: The identity of the node to be deleted.

Program Output: A printout of the data fields of all the nodes of the modified list.

(7-P10) Write a program that deletes the first *n* elements of a linked list.

User Input: *n*.

Program Output: A printout of the data fields of all the nodes of the modified list.

PROGRAM FOR CHAPTER SEVEN

Program 7.1: Structs and a Linked List

```
      #include<stdlib.h>
      #include<stdio.h>
      #include<string.h>

[1] struct vehicle
      {
         char            name[15];
         char            ident[10];
         float           price;
         int             doors;
         struct vehicle  *next;
      };

[2] typedef struct vehicle NODE;
```

```
         void print_list(NODE *);
         void assign_values(NODE *);
         void create_header(NODE *);

         main()
         {
           NODE    *p, *q, *start;    /* these are the pointers! */

           int     sentinel = 1;

[3]        start = (NODE *)malloc(sizeof(NODE));
[4]        create_header(start);
           p = start;

           while (sentinel != 0)
             {
[5]            q = p;
[6]            p = (NODE *) malloc(sizeof(NODE));
[7]            q->next = p;
               assign_values(p);
               printf("More entries?  [0 to end, 1 to continue].... \n ");
               scanf("%d", &sentinel);
             }

           p->next = NULL;
           print_list(start);
         }

         void create_header(NODE *ptr)
           {
             strncpy(ptr->name, "CarList", sizeof("CarList"));
             strncpy(ptr->ident, "Head", sizeof("Head"));
             ptr->price = 0.0;
             ptr->doors = 0;
           }

         void assign_values(NODE *pt)
           {
             printf("Enter the name and the ID code. \n");
             scanf("%s %s", &(pt->name), &(pt->ident));
             printf("Enter the price and number of doors. \n");
             scanf("%f %d", &(pt->price), &(pt->doors));
           }

         void print_list(NODE *pt)
           {
            while (pt != NULL)
              {
                printf("%s \n", pt->name);
                pt = pt->next;
              }
           }
```

8   Files

This short chapter has a very practical goal: to enable us to use data stored outside the main memory as input to a program. There are two reasons for doing this. First, using external storage as a source of input data saves us the trouble of typing the input over and over should we decide to run a program multiple times. Second, an ordinary editor can be used to type the data and store them on the external device.

The programming construct that enables all this is the file. We can define a *file* as a named collection of data that is stored *outside* the computer's memory. To a C system, this collection is nothing more than a stream of bytes, one after the other. To a program, the bytes might very well be related. Figure 8.1 shows a hypothetical stream of 16 bytes viewed by two different programs. In part (a), it is viewed as a sequence of four groups of bytes, with each group itself composed of two subgroups of two bytes each. Perhaps each subgroup is an integer; the file could then represent a set of four coordinates on a computer screen. In part (b), each byte is considered a separate entity. If, in the latter case, each byte is treated as an ASCII character, the file is known as a *text file*. In this chapter, we will be exploring text files.

Since files are stored outside the memory, they remain intact even after the computer is turned off. Also, a file can be very large, since external storage devices are huge compared to a computer's main memory. However, files confront us with an is-

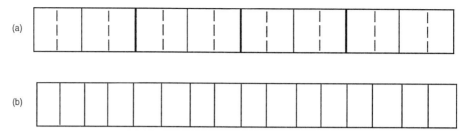

Figure 8.1   Schematic representations of two differently organized files.

sue we have not faced before: the transfer of data between external storage[1] and main memory. There are two kinds of data transfers:

Reading. This is the term we use to describe input from a file. We used the same term to describe input from the keyboard. Data are transferred from disk to memory.

Writing. This is the term we use to describe output to a file. We used the same term to describe output to the screen. Data are transferred from memory to disk.

Programs 8.1 and 8.2 involve the use of text files. The first illustrates how one integer at a time is read from a file. The second does not involve any new principles beyond those used in the first. It simply illustrates how to create the same linked list used in Program 7.1, only with data gotten from a file. It is summarized at the end of the chapter.

8.1

FILE BUFFERS

The data that comprise a file are not necessarily found in one contiguous area of the disk. Rather, they are often scattered in a number of distinct areas (Figure 8.2, shaded areas). In order for the disk system to access an entire file, it often needs to scan a large part of the surface of a disk. It does this with a magnetic sensor called a *head*, a device that can be guided to access any area on the disk. Head movement, although fast by human standards, is extremely slow to a computer, which can process many lines of a program in the time it takes to move the head even a little. Clearly, something must get done behind the scenes to collect the scattered data so that a programmer thinks they are all a single entity.

What gets done is this: the computer creates a buffer for file data. When a program requires input from the file, the computer loads data from the various parts of the disk into the buffer. Then the program reads from the buffer, rather than the disk. Since the file is a text file, the buffer contains a sequence of individual ASCII characters. Note that this is precisely the situation for keyboard input: The program reads a buffer containing individual ASCII characters. We can conclude, then, that the proc-

---

1 From this point on, we will assume that external storage is some sort of disk system.

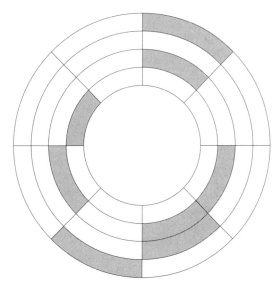

Figure 8.2   Surface of a disk. Shaded segments taken together comprise a single file.

essing of characters from a file buffer is exactly the same as the processing of characters from a keyboard buffer. Put another way, a line of input from a text file is treated
precisely the same way by a program as a line of input from the keyboard.

Since we have studied the underlying principles in the keyboard case, we won't
repeat ourselves for the file case. However, we do need to learn all the commands
that direct the computer to deal with the file buffer, rather than the keyboard buffer.

8.2

FILE COMMANDS

Regardless of the type of computer system, reading or writing a text file involves
three basic steps:

1. Opening the file: This step signals the computer that a particular file is
needed. The computer sets up a buffer for that file, creates a pointer called a *file descriptor,* which enables the system to locate the buffer, and associates the file descriptor with the file name. *All subsequent file commands reference the file descriptor, not
the file name.*

2. Transferring the data: This step takes care of the actual movement of data
between main memory and file buffer.

3. Closing the file: This step tells the computer that the file is no longer needed.
Closing a file frees the buffer for possible future use. (A computer may allow only a
certain number of buffers to be in use at any one time; so it makes sense to close a

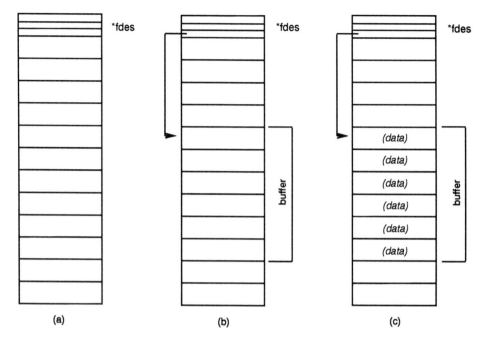

Figure 8.3   Schematic diagram memory during file I/O. (1) File is declared. (2) File is opened. (3) Data are read in.

file when it is no longer needed.) In the case of writing, there is an additional reason to close a file: The computer transfers to disk any data remaining in the buffer.

Let us look now at the actual *C* code needed to read a single integer from a file of integers (**test.dat**) and store it in a given location (**cars**). The three parts of Figure 8.3 show a schematic diagram of the memory after the first three steps below have been executed.

- **Step 1:** Declare a file descriptor (Figure 8.3a):

```
FILE    *fdes;
```

Here, we have chosen **fdes** as the file descriptor. It is a pointer to a structure whose predefined type name is **FILE**. Thus ***fdes** is the structure. One of its members is a pointer to the buffer that will be used for the data transfers. Note that the keyword **FILE** must be in uppercase characters. In general, a file declaration looks like this:

```
FILE    *<file descriptor>;
```

A declaration of a file descriptor appears in line [1] of Program 8.1, and line [1] of Program 8.2.

- **Step 2:** Open the file (Figure 8.3b):

```
fdes = fopen("test.dat", "r");
```

The function `fopen` returns a pointer to the buffer set up for `test.dat`. In the above case, the returned value is stored somewhere in `*fdes`. The `"r"` indicates that we wish to read the file; the `test.dat` is the file to be read. In general, the command to open a file for reading looks like this:

```
<file descriptor> = fopen("<file name>","r");
```

A statement opening a file appears in line [2] of Program 8.1, and line [2] of Program 8.2.

- **Step 3:** Read the file (Figure 8.3c):

```
fscanf(fdes, "%d", &cars);
```

This tells the system to read an integer from the buffer pointed to by `*fdes` and store it at the address `cars`.

Note that this looks almost like `scanf`; the difference is the presence of `fdes`. Most important, it *works* like `scanf`, but it reads the file buffer, not the keyboard buffer. Recall that this involves converting digits (characters) to the indicated data type. As with `scanf`, there is an internal position indicator to keep track of the next character to be read. In general, the `fscanf` statement looks like this:

```
fscanf(<file descriptor>, "<control string>", <addresses>);
```

A file read statement can be seen in line [3] of Program 8.1. Two file read statements appear in line [7] of Program 8.2. The first reads a pair of strings, while the second reads a floating point number and an integer.

- **Step 4:** Close the file:

```
fclose(fdes);
```

In general, the file close statement looks like this:

```
fclose(<file descriptor>);
```

A file close statement appears in line [5] of Program 8.1, and line [6] of Program 8.2.

8.2.1 Detecting the End of a File

In Program 8.1 we deal with a file of many integers, not just one. Furthermore, the number of integers in the file is unknown to us (which is usually the case, by the way). How, then, can we know if we have reached the end of the file? Fortunately, the end of a file is marked by a so-called *end of file indicator*. It is possible to test for this indicator using the expression `feof(fdes)`, assuming that `fdes` is the name of the file descriptor. This expression returns an answer to the question: *Did we come to the end of the file at the last input statement?* It is normally used as the condition in a `while` loop header; the body of the loop contains a statement that reads the file. Such a loop is illustrated in line [4] of Program 8.1, and line [4] of Program 8.2. As long as the end of the file has not been reached, `feof` evaluates to *false*, and the `while` condition evaluates to *true*. When the end of the file is reached, `feof` returns *true*, and the `while` condition becomes *false*.

Summary of Program 8.1

Strategy: This code reads a file of integers, and prints out each one immediately after it is read. Lines [1] and [2] declare a file descriptor and open the file. Line [4] is a **while** loop that reads and prints, using **feof** to test for the end of the file at each iteration. It is important to realize that the reading of the last data item does not change the value of **feof(fdes)**. Only after an attempt has been made to read the end of file indicator itself does **feof(fdes)** change. Because of this, it is advisable to make the **fscanf** line the last statement in the loop. By doing this, it is assured that immediately after the end of file indicator is read, the loop will stop executing. This is as it should be; when all the data in the file are exhausted, no more file processing should take place.

Since the loop both reads and prints, and the read must come last, we have no choice but to put **printf** before **scanf**. Thus we need to put a **scanf** outside the loop (line [3]), so that when the loop is initially entered, the first integer read will be printed. Experiment 8-1 will explore the question of reading first versus printing first.

Style: The file is closed after it is no longer needed.

EXPERIMENT 8-1

Using a text editor, create a text file **ints.dat** like the one below.

```
33 27
121
41 83 26
```

Leave only one space between the numbers on a line, and hit **ENTER** after the end of each line. Modify the code of Program 8.1 as follows: switch the order of the two statements in the **while** loop, and eliminate the **fscanf** statement that is outside the loop. Run the program and examine the output. Explain the results.

EXPERIMENT 8-2

Use the file **ints.dat** for this experiment. Use the original code that reads **ints.dat** (before it was modified as in the last experiment). Declare **ch** as a character, and modify the code this way:

```
fscanf statements: ---> fscanf(fdes, "%c",&ch);
printf statement:   ---> printf("%c \n", ch);
```

Run the program. Explain why a line is skipped after the **27** and **121** are printed. Hint: What does this say about the way **scanf** treats the **newline** character?

Summary of Program 8.2

Strategy: In this program, we make a linked list essentially as in Program 7.1. Thus most of the statements in the program should seem familiar. The main difference is that the data come from a file called "linkdata." In line [1] the file descriptor is declared; in line [2] the file is opened. Line [3] calls a function to create the header node. After this, the main loop is entered (line [4]). As in Program 7.1, this loop is where much of the list is created. The file reading takes place in the function `assign_values`, which reads data for the four members of a node directly from the file. When this function reads the end of file indicator, the program exits from the loop. Note that since the loop creates a node first, then fills it with data, the last node has no meaningful data, since `assign_values` read the end of file indicator. Line [5] takes this into account; it puts the null pointer in the next to the last node, rather than the last one.

Style: The file descriptor is made global so all functions can access it.

Exercises

(8-1) Consider the buffer below (assume it is pointed to by `f`):

1	2	.	4		A	2	8				6	4	D	<end of file>

What are the values of the variables after each of these `fscanf` statements executes? Assume each statement executes just after the file is opened. For each case, indicate where the position indicator ends up.

```
1 - fscanf(f, "%c %c",& ch1, &ch2);
2 - fscanf(f, "%f %c", &r, &ch1);
3 - fscanf(f, "%f %c", &r, &ch1);
4 - fscanf(f, "%f %c %d", &r, &ch1, &i1);
5 - fscanf(f, "%f %c %d %d", &r, &ch1, &i1, &i2);
6 - while ( !feof(f) )
          fscanf(f, "%c", &ch1);
```

(8-2) How many files can be simultaneously open in your computer system?

Creating Text Files

The idea that a data file can be created using an ordinary editor is something we have been touting as a great boon. Certainly it is a convenient way to produce a data file. However, this is not the only way. Sometimes we need to create a text file from within a program. The code to do this looks very similar to the code for reading a file:

```
int     count;
FILE    *fdes;

fdes = fopen("ints.dat","w");
for (count = 1; count <= 20; count++)
    fprintf(fdes, "%d \n", count);
fclose(fdes);
```

There are two main differences between this and the code to read a text file:

1. We use `fopen` with the code "w" for `write`. This instructs the computer to create a new file into which we shall write data.

2. The statement for doing the actual writing is `fprintf`, which is analogous to `printf` except it writes the integers to the buffer pointed to by `*fdes`, rather than the screen.

Since this code creates a new file, we do not need to look for the end of the file. Hence, we can use a loop that executes a predetermined number of times.

Programming Problems

NOTE: Each of the problems in this section requires manipulation of a text file. It is assumed that a suitable text file already exists. If that is not the case, one can easily be created using a text editor.

(8-P1) Write a program that copies every other character of a text file into another text file.

User Input: The names of two text files.

Program Output: A printout of the contents of the new file.

(8-P2) Write a program that merges two text files into a third by alternately writing a word from each file into the third. When the contents of one file are exhausted, the remainder of the second is written to the third.

User Input: The names of three text files.

Program Output: A printout of the contents of the merged file.

(8-P3) Write a program that reads a file of integers and prints only those numbers that exceed the average of the numbers in the file.

User Input: A file name.

Program Output: The average of the numbers in the file; a list of all numbers greater than the average.

(8-P4) Consider this declaration:

```
struct employee
  {
     int      age;
     float    salary;
  };


typedef employee EMPLOYEE;
```

Write a program that reads a file consisting of alternating integers and real numbers (corresponding to ages and salaries) and creates an array of structs as above. Assume that there are 100 employees at most.

User Input: A filename.

Program Output: The statement *The table of ages and salaries has been successfully completed.*

(8-P4) Using the same struct as above, write a program which finds the average salary of all employees over the age of 40. Assume that there are 100 employees.

User Input: A filename.

Program Output: The statement *The average salary of all employees over the age of XX is YY.*, where *XX* and *YY* are replaced accordingly.

(8-P5) A consumer group decides to test twelve high-priced car batteries that are claimed to have unusual cold-start power. They do their tests on a particularly cold day, and measure the amount of current each battery can deliver. They store these data in a text file. Write a program to display selected results of this test.

User Input: A choice of (a) or (b).

(a) The brand name of the battery whose current is desired.

(b) A request for the identity of the best battery.

Program Output: A menu prompting the user to select one of the above, or to quit. For (a), the amount of current produced by the given battery. For (b), the identity of the battery that produced the most current. The program should return to the menu after completing a calculation.

(8-P6) Write a program that reads a text file and counts the total number of vowels.

User Input: A text file name.

Program Output: The statement `The total number of vowels in file XXX is YYY`, where `XXX` is the file name, and `YYY` is the total number of vowels.

(8-P7) Write a program that reads a text file, encrypts it into a "secret" code, then writes the result to another file. (Hint: Review Experiment 2-1.)

User Input: A text file name.

Program Output: (a) A new file called `code.dat`, which is the encrypted file. (b) A message output to the screen indicating that the job has been done. If the input file could not be opened, a message should indicate that.

PROGRAMS FOR CHAPTER EIGHT

Program 8.1: Reading a File of Integers

```
           #include<sstudio.h>
           main()
             {
[1]            FILE *fdes;
               int  x;

[2]            fdes = fopen("test.dat", "r");
[3]            fscanf(fdes, "%d", &x);

[4]            while(!feof(fdes) )
                 {
                    printf("Value is %d \n", x);
                 }
[5]            fclose(fdes);
             }
```

Program 8.2: Reading a File of structs

```
           #include<stdlib.h>
           #include<stdio.h>
           #include<string.h>

           struct vehicle
             {
                char              name[15];
                char              ident[10];
                float             price;
                int               doors;
                struct vehicle    *next;
             };

           typedef struct vehicle NODE;
```

```
[1] FILE    *infile;

    void print_list(NODE *);
    void assign_values(NODE *);
    void create_header(NODE *);

    main()
      {
        NODE    *p, *q, *start;

[2]     infile = fopen("linkdata", "r");

        start = (NODE *)malloc(sizeof(NODE));
[3]     create_header(start);
        p = start;

[4]     while ( !feof(infile) )
          {
            q = p;
            p = (NODE *) malloc(sizeof(NODE));
            q->next = p;
            assign_values(p);
          }

[5]   q->next = NULL;
      free(p->next);
[6]   fclose(infile);
      print_list(start);
    }

    void create_header(NODE *ptr)
      {
        strncpy(ptr->name, "LIST",  sizeof("LIST"));
        strncpy(ptr->ident, "HEAD", sizeof("HEAD"));
        ptr->price = 0.0;
        ptr->doors = 0;
      }

[7] void assign_values(NODE *pt)
      {
        fscanf(infile, "%s %s", &(pt->name), &(pt->ident));
        fscanf(infile, "%f %d", &(pt->price), &(pt->doors));
      }

    void print_list(NODE *pt)
      {
        while (pt != NULL)
          {
            printf("%s \n", pt->name);
            pt = pt->next;
          }
      }
```

9 Recursion

Suppose we have some money invested in a stock, and we follow closely its ups and downs in the stock market. To get the current price of a stock, we leave this message for our friendly broker, Frank: *What's the share price of Wiggy Industries?* Just this day, Frank doesn't know. He calls his trustworthy colleague, Phyllis, and leaves her the same message: *What's the share price of Wiggy Industries?* Sad to say, Phyllis is behind in her work today and doesn't have the price at hand. Not to worry! Phyllis has an extremely reliable friend, Nora, who gets her information directly from a stock ticker in her office. *Nora, what's the share price of Wiggy Industries?* Nora answers Phyllis at once: *The price is $23.55.* Phyllis relays the answer to Frank: *The price is $23.55.* Frank, in turn, now leaves a message with us: *The price is $23.55.* We, of course, are completely unaware of this chain of events; as far as we are concerned, we asked a question, and we got our answer.

At each step of the above process, someone attempts to find out the price of a stock. Let us imagine that we have a C function designed to mimic this attempt. Its input is an inquiry about the price, and its output is the answer. Such a function would look essentially like this:

```
Function inquire:
    if (<price is known>)
        answer = price;
    else   <invoke inquire>;
    return (answer);
```

This two-line function seems simple enough: If the price is known right away, **answer** is assigned **price**, the **else** clause is bypassed, and **answer** is returned to the caller. However, if the price is *not* known, a strange thing happens: the **else** clause calls **inquire**. That is, the function calls itself! We have never done anything like this before. The act of a function calling itself is known as *recursion*. In Figure 9.1, we have attempted to recreate the above phone calling scenario in terms of recursive calls to **inquire**. In the diagram, each box represents an invocation of the function **inquire**. Let us look at the process from start to finish:

(a) The first box represents our initial desire to determine the price of the stock. Since the **if** condition is not answered in the affirmative, the **else** clause invokes **inquire** with a call to Frank. Note that the **if-else** statement has not finished, and the **return(answer)** statement has not even been started.

(b) The second box represents Frank's invocation of **inquire**. He doesn't know the price, so the **else** clause in his box invokes **inquire** with a call to Phyllis. Note that Frank's **if-else** statement has not been completed, nor has his **return(answer)** statement been started.

(c) This box represents Phyllis' invocation of **inquire**. Her **if-else** cannot be answered in the affirmative; so her **else** clause invokes **inquire** with a call to Nora. Once again, an **if-else** has not gone to completion, and the **return(answer)** has not been started.

(d) This box represents Nora's invocation of **inquire**. Here something different happens. Nora's **if** clause turns out to be *true;* so **answer** is assigned a value (no further calls to **inquire** are needed), and the **return(answer)** statement executes. This is the first invocation of **inquire** that has gone to completion. Now the previous invocation of **inquire** is resumed at the point where it left off: somewhere in Phyllis' **if-else** statement. That statement can now finish executing because its call to **inquire** is complete. Also, since the value of **answer** was passed from Nora to

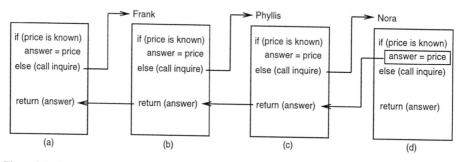

Figure 9.1   Evolution of calls to **inquire** routine.

Phyllis by Nora's `return` statement, Phyllis' `return(answer)` statement can execute. With Phyllis' invocation of `inquire` now being complete, the previous one (Frank's) can pick up where it left off: somewhere in his `if-else` statement. Frank's `if-else` now completes, his `return(answer)` statement executes (`answer` being known since it was passed back by Phyllis), and his call to `inquire` is complete. Finally, the previous call (the original one) picks up where it left off: at the `if-else` statement. This `if-else` goes to completion, and the answer is returned to us.

We cannot have a function call itself anytime we please. When a function calls itself, it must not only follow the usual rules of a function call, using the correct number, type, and order of parameters, it must meet two additional conditions:

1. There must ultimately be an instance where the function no longer needs to call itself. This is referred to as the *base case*. In our example, Nora was the base case. After the call to Nora was made, no further calls were necessary.

2. Each recursive call must leave a problem that is simpler, or closer to the solution, than the existing problem. This is the case in our example: There is a list of people to call, and with each call the list gets shorter.

An Easy Recursion Example

Suppose we need a function that evaluates expressions of the form x^y, where both x and y are integers. We know that x must be multiplied by itself y times. Certainly, we could put a product expression in a loop, and let the loop execute y times. We can also solve the problem without any loops. Consider the following function, defined in Program 9.1:

```
int power(int x, int y)
{
    if ( y == 1 )
        return(x);
    else return( x * power(x, y-1) );
}
```

Clearly, this function is recursive. Furthermore, it obeys the rules about recursion. Each recursive call to the function leaves a smaller problem (the calculation of a smaller power of **x**), and there is a base case (the function returns an answer when the exponent is 1). Figure 9.2 shows how the function works for a call of `power(4,4)`.

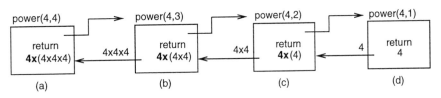

Figure 9.2   Evolution of calls to `power(4,4)` function.

1. First the call to `power(4,4)` (Figure 9.2a). Since `y` starts out as `4`, the `if` statement cannot be completed. It is left trying to calculate `4` times the result of a call to `power(4,3)`.

2. Now the call to `power(4,3)` (Figure 9.2b). Since `y` is `3`, this call cannot be completed either. It is left trying to calculate `4` times `power(4,2)`.

3. Next, the call to `power(4,2)` (Figure 9.2c). The exponent is still not `1`, so the third call is left trying to calculate the product of `4` and `power(4,1)`.

4. This call is the base case (Figure 9.2d). Since `y` is now `1`, a value of `4` is returned to the most recent call: `power(4,2)`.

5. The call `power(4,2)` takes the `4` returned to it, multiplies it by `4`, and returns a `16` to the most recent call: `power(4,3)`.

6. The call `power(4,3)` takes the `16` returned to it, multiplies it by `4`, and returns a `64` to the most recent call: `power(4,4)`.

7. Finally, the original call can complete. The `64` returned to it is multiplied by `4` and the answer is obtained.

Except for the mechanics of calculating an answer, this problem is identical to the call–return sequence described in the telephone example. In effect, we agree to solve the problem `power(4,4)` provided Frank solves `power(4,3)`. Frank agrees to solve `power(4,3)` provided Phyllis solves `power(4,2)`. Phyllis agrees to do `power(4,2)`, provided Nora gives her the answer to `power(4,1)`. Since Nora can easily solve her problem without anyone's help, she can return her part of the answer to Phyllis, who returns her part of the answer to Frank, who returns his part of the answer to us. Thus the problem is solved.

EXPERIMENT 9-1

(a) Run Program 9.1 for convincing evidence that recursion actually works. Then run it again, except have the `else` part return `power(x,y-1)` without multiplying it by `x`. Explain the difference by tracing the calls using a diagram similar to that of Figure 9.2. Suggestion: make the power different from the base.

(b) Is it just as effective to reduce the "size" of each call by using `power(x-1,y)` in the `else` part? What happens?

A Difficult Recursion Example

Having done an easy problem, we will now do one that at first glance seems almost impossible. With recursion, however, the solution is remarkably simple. The problem is an ancient puzzle called the *Tower of Hanoi*. The puzzle itself is straightforward. There are three vertical pegs and a large number of discs set up as in Figure 9.3

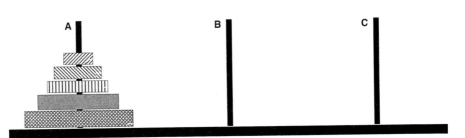

Figure 9.3   Tower of Hanoi Puzzle.

(which has only five discs for clarity). The goal is to transfer the pile of discs from peg A to peg C, subject to these rules:

- Only one disc at a time may be moved.
- A larger disc may not be put on top of a smaller one.

The program we write must print out a set of instructions detailing each move needed to accomplish the transfer.

Let's try to gain some understanding by looking at a Tower with fewer discs. Obviously, the one-disc problem is trivial. We will therefore start with a two-disc Tower (Figure 9.4). It is easy to see that these steps solve that problem:

1. Move top disc from A to B (Figure 9.4b).
2. Move bottom disc from A to C (Figure 9.4c).
3. Move top disc from B to C (Figure 9.4d).

Believe it or not, we've just done a major part of the work! We now know how to move two discs from A to C. However, we haven't described the solution in suffi-

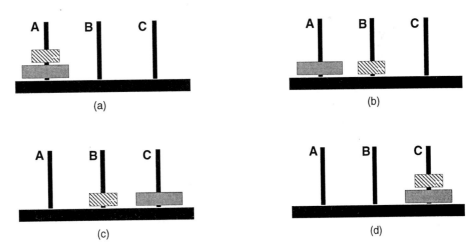

Figure 9.4   Solving the two disc Tower of Hanoi problem.

ciently general terms. Suppose the two discs had been on B, and we were asked to move them to A. The *principles* for doing so are embodied in the above recipe, but the *details* are wrong because of the labeling. We can correct this (minor) problem by relabeling the pegs:

> The peg holding the original pile will be called the source and labeled `source`.

> The peg where we want the pile to end up will be called the destination, and labeled `dest`.

> The unused peg will be labeled `temp`.

Note that A, B, and C can each be `source,` `destination,` or `temp`, depending on how the problem is set up. Using the new terminology, the recipe looks like this:

Recipe I:

1. Move top disc from `source` to `temp`.
2. Move bottom disc from `source` to `dest`.
3. Move top disc from `temp` to `dest`.

Now we have truly solved the problem of moving two discs from any one peg to any other peg.

Let's move on to three discs. We have drawn these in Figure 9.5 so that the top two look like a single "package." Once again, the goal is to move these three from A to C. In our new parlance, `source` = A, `dest` = C, and `temp` = B. To solve the problem, we will cheat a little, temporarily suspending the rules about moving one at a time. Then we can use this recipe:

Recipe II:

1. Move top "package" from `source` to `temp`.
2. Move bottom disc from `source` to `dest`.
3. Move top "package" from `temp` to `dest`.

Note that this is basically the same solution as Recipe I—not surprising, since we are treating this situation as if there were only two discs. Of course, steps (1) and (3) violate the original rules: They move more than one disc at a time. But look carefully at step (1). It calls for moving two discs from one peg to another. *We already know how to do that.* Step (3) calls for the same thing. We can therefore reinstate the rule about moving one disc at a time, and still follow the above recipe. All we have to do is invoke the two disc solution every time the instruction calls for moving a "package."

We now know how to solve the three-disc problem. At the risk of being repetitious, we'll look briefly at the four-disc case, after which we should be able to see the

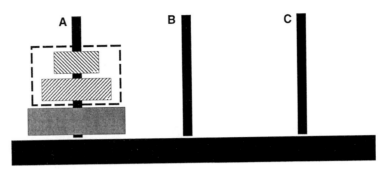

Figure 9.5   Solving the three disc Tower of Hanoi problem.

pattern. Once again, we consider the four discs as a three-disc package on top of a single disc. This problem is solved by Recipe II, since it consists of a disc with a package on top. Of course, a package has three discs in this case, but that's no problem; we know how to move three discs from one peg to another. All we have to do is invoke the three-disc solution every time the instruction calls for moving a package. Therefore, we can solve the four-disc problem.

We can extend this logic for as many discs as we like. That should convince us the solution is recursive. For example, suppose someone is asked to solve the four-disc case. He declares: "I will solve this problem if you let me consider the top three discs as a single package. Frank will take care of the package." Frank agrees: "I will solve the three-disc problem if you let me consider the top two as a package, and let Phyllis deal with the two-disc case." Phyllis agrees; having read this book, she knows how to solve the two-disc problem without help from anyone else. We can see that this process follows the pattern of both the `inquire` and `power` problems. Each step reduces the problem to a smaller version of the previous one. Furthermore, there is a base case.

What should the actual routine look like? The function defined in Program 9.2 illustrates (`n` is the number of discs):

```
void tower(int n, char source, char dest, char temp)
{
  if n > 0
    {
      tower(n-1, source, temp,  dest);
      printf("Move top disc from %c to %c. \n", source, dest);
      tower(n-1, temp, dest, source);
    }
}
```

It should come as no surprise that there are three statements, one for each of the steps in Recipe II. The first and third steps are the programming equivalent of *move the package*, which is a request to solve the next smaller size problem. Hence the recursive call. The second step is the equivalent of moving the remaining disk after the package has been lifted off.

The hard part is to understand why the parameters in the recursive calls are in the order shown. To solve the original problem, we initially call `tower(n,a,b,c)`. Note that we are using the labeling of Figure 9.5: `a` is `source`, `b` is `temp`, and `c` is `dest`. Now, step (1) of the recipe says to transfer the package from `a` to `b`. Therefore, in the first recursive call, the destination is the peg we labeled `temp` in Figure 9.5. The source is the peg we labeled `source`, while the unused peg is the one we labeled `dest`. Hence in the first recursive call, the order of the parameters is `source`, `temp`, `dest`. Step (3) of the recipe says to transfer the package from `b` to `c`. Therefore, in the second recursive call, the source is the peg we originally labeled `temp`, the destination is the peg we labeled `dest`, while the peg we labeled `source` is unused here. Hence, the order of the parameters must be `temp`, `dest`, `source`. As for step (2), this says to move the lone disc from the peg labeled `source` to the peg labeled `dest`. The `printf` statement simply prints this instruction, since there is no problem moving one disc.

Exercises

(9-1) Consider an unknown function `f(n)`, where `n` is an integer. Suppose that all we know are these two facts:

```
(a)   f(0) = 1
(b)   f(n) = n*f(n-1),    n >= 1
```

Part (b) defines what is called a *recursion relation*, one where the value of a given term depends on the value of one or more prior terms. After convincing yourself that the two requirements for writing a recursive routine are satisfied, write a recursive routine to calculate f(n). Then calculate f(2) through f(5).

(9-2) Suppose that in Exercise 9-1, the base case had been given a value of 2, not 1. What effect would that have on the operation of the recursive function? What if the base case had a value of 0?

(9-3) Consider the recursion relation

$$f(n+1) = n*f(n-1) + (n-1)*f(n), n \geq 1$$

What is the minimum amount of information you need, besides this formula, in order to write a successful recursive routine to calculate f?

(9-4) What does the evolution of the calls look like for the Tower of Hanoi N = 3 case? Draw a diagram similar to Figure 9.1.

(9-5) Suppose the order of the parameters in the header of function `tower` changes to `temp, source, dest`. How would the order of the parameters in the recursive calls change?

NOTE: For the next two problems, draw a linked list with nodes comprising two members: **data**, containing an integer, and **ptr**, containing a pointer to the next node. Assume the first node is pointed to by **start**.

(9-6) Study each of these two routines carefully. First, figure out what they are supposed to do. Then determine which one will work, which won't (and why it won't).

```
int  prob96a(NODE p)       /* invoke: prob96a(start) */
{
    if (p == NULL)
    return 0;
    else return p->data + prob96a(p->ptr);
}

int  prob96b(NODE first, NODE p)  /* invoke: prob96b(start,start) */
{
    p = first;
    if (p == NULL)
    return 0;
    else return p->data + prob96b(p, p->ptr);
}
```

(9-7) Follow the instructions given in the previous problem.

```
int  prob97a(NODE p)             /* invoke: prob97a(start) */
{
    if (p != NULL)
    return 2*prob97a(p->ptr);
    else return 0;
}

int  prob97b(NODE p)             /* invoke: prob97b(start) */
{
    if (p != NULL)
    return 2*prob97b(p->ptr);
    else return prob97b(p->data);
}
```

(9-8) Given the function below, trace the evolution of the recursive calls when the value **4** is passed to it. Use a diagram in the spirit of Figure 9.2.

```
int  prob98(int x)
{
    if( (x == 0) || (x == 1) )
        return x;
    else return prob98(x - 1)*prob98(x - 2);
}
```

Programming Problems

(9-P1) Many sequences of numbers have a kind of regularity that enables one to predict the value of any term. For example, if S_n denotes any term in this sequence:

$$0, \; 1, \; 4, \; 9, \; 16, \; 25, \; 36, \; 49, \; 64, \; 81, \; ...$$

then we can say that $S_n = n^2$, where n denotes the n-th term of the sequence (we start counting with n = 0). For other sequences, prediction is not as straightforward. For example, this sequence:

$$1, \; 1, \; 2, \; 3, \; 5, \; 8, \; 13, \; 21, \; 34, \; 55, \; ...$$

can be characterized in this way: $S_n = S_{n-1} + S_{n-2}$, $n \geq 2$. Note that it gives the value of any member of the sequence (beyond the second) only in terms of other members of the sequence. This formula is called a *recursion relation*. Like the recursive solution we discussed in the chapter, this solution is expressed in terms of solutions to "smaller" problems. For each of the formulas listed below, write a recursive function that implements the relation. Write a program to test the function with several values of n. (Pick a reasonable base case for each.)

(a) $S_n = 2 * S_{n-1}$

(b) $S_n = n * S_{n-1}$

(c) $S_n = n * S_{n-1} + 2$

(d) $S_n = n * S_{n-1} + n$

User Input: None. The parameters to the function are coded into the program.

Program Output: The value returned by the function.

(9-P2) Converting a number from our conventional system (called base 10) to the binary system (called base 2)[1] involves a process of repeated integer division, discarding quotients, but keeping remainders. The process stops when the quotient is 0. This example illustrates:

To convert 11 to its base 2 equivalent:

$$11 \div 2 = 5; \text{remainder} = 1$$
$$5 \div 2 = 2; \text{remainder} = 1$$
$$2 \div 2 = 1; \text{remainder} = 0$$
$$1 \div 2 = 0; \text{remainder} = 1$$

The base 2 equivalent is the sequence of remainders *in the reverse order:* 1 0 1 1.

Write a recursive function that converts any positive integer to its base 2 equivalent.

---

1 Relax. You don't have to know anything about the binary system to do this program.

User Input: A positive base 10 integer, n.

Program Output: The base 2 equivalent of n.

(9-P3) Write a program that reverses the elements of a linked list.

User Input: None. A pointer to the beginning of a linked list is coded into the program.

Program Output: The original list, and the list in reverse order.

(9-P4) Write a recursive function that calculates the factorial of a number.

Function Input: The integer whose factorial is to be calculated.

Function Output: The factorial of the input.

PROGRAMS FOR CHAPTER NINE

Program 9.1: A Power Function Using Recursion.

```
#include<stdio.h>
main()
{
 int  power(int, int);

 printf("The value of %d to the power %d is %d \n", 4, 4,
        ' power(4,4));
}

int  power(int x, int y)
{
  if (y==1)
    return(x);
  else return( x*power(x,y-1));
}
```

Program 9.2: The Tower of Hanoi

```
#include<stdio.h>
main()
{
 void tower(int, char, char, char);

 tower(3, 'A', 'B', 'C');
}
```

```
void tower(int n, char source, char dest, char temp)
{
  if (n > 0)
    {
      tower(n-1, source, temp, dest);
      printf("Move top disc from %c to %c. \n", source, dest);
      tower(n-1, temp, dest, source);
    }
}
```

10 Optional Extras

For readers who have the time and the desire, we present a variety of topics that go beyond the realm of introduction. All should be reasonably within reach, although Section 10.7 is considerably more advanced than the others. There is no significance to the order given. However, Section 10.3 should be studied prior to Section 10.7.

10.1

ADDITIONAL DATA TYPES

So far, we have been able to convey all the ideas we need using only three data types: `int`, `char`, and `float`. However, there are times when other types are useful. Recall that a data type essentially tells the computer how to interpret the bit combination at a particular location. For numbers, the interpretation is dictated by the rules of binary arithmetic. Those rules tell us, for example, that the size of the largest integer that can be represented increases with the number of bytes used. Two-byte integers (we really mean *signed* integers, since both negative and positive values are included) can represent values in the range approximately ±32,000; four-byte integers can represent values in the range of about $\pm 2 \times 10^9$. One might think, then, that a computer would use the largest feasible number of bytes for its integers. Such integers, however, are not always the most advantageous. Calculations with one-byte integers (range: [−127,128]) can be done with greater speed than the same calculations with two- or four-byte integers. For the most versatility, then, several types of integers should be provided.[1] In *C*, there are three types of (signed) integers: `int`, `longint` (more bytes than `int`), and `short` (a single byte).

One extra type we introduced previously was the unsigned integer. We described it as a positive integer that is used in situations where negative values make no sense. Such an integer is represented differently from a normal integer. Since every value is positive, there is no need to use any bits to account for a sign. Thus, for example, a sixteen-bit unsigned integer will range from 0 to about 64,000. *C* has both `unsigned` and `unsigned long` (same idea as before: more bytes than `unsigned`).

For floating point numbers, things get a little more complicated. Not only is the largest absolute value dependent on the number of bits, so is its *precision* (the number of places to the right of the decimal point). The type `double` declares a variable that uses more bytes than the type `float`; the type `long double`, more still.

The table below is a list of data types available in *C*, along with their format specifiers. The order of the entries in the table tells us about how the compiler does data type promotion. If an expression has mixed data types, then *C* will promote each variable in the expression to the type that is highest on the list.

Data Type	Format Specifier
long double	%Lf
double	%lf
float	%f
unsigned long int	%lu
long int	%ld
unsigned int	%u
int	%d
short	%hd
char	%c

Example: Data Type Promotion

All terms in the expression in the `printf` statement below get promoted to type `double`.

```
int      a;
float    b;
short    c;
double   d;

printf("The sum of these numbers is %lf \n", a + b + c + d);
```

---

[1] The exact number of bytes for these type can vary with machine.

10.2

SHORTHAND OPERATOR NOTATION

It is often the case that we wish to add a quantity q to a variable x. Until now, we would do this with expressions of the form x = x ± q. In *C*, there is the following shorthand notation:

```
x += q or x -= q
```

Experienced programmers usually prefer the shorthand version. It is easier to write, and is easily remembered as, "increase x by q" or "decrease x by q," depending on the sign. The table below summarizes other shorthand operator notation.

Short Notation	Long Notation
x += q	x = x + q
x -= q	x = x - q
x *= q	x = x * q
x /= q	x = x / q
x %= q	x = x % q

Increment and Decrement Operators

An even briefer shorthand is used when the value of q in the foregoing expressions is 1. In Chapter 3, we wrote the `for` loop's increment rule as n++ rather than n = n + 1. The ++ is called the *increment operator*. It is a unary operator that, when placed before or after a variable, adds 1 to the current value of the variable. For example, each of these statements:

```
n++;
++n;
```

causes the value of n to increase by one.

The reason why the increment operator is interesting will become evident after the following experiment:

EXPERIMENT 10-1:

Declare two integers a and b, initializing each to 1. Run a short program with this statement:

```
printf("%d  %d \n", b++, ++a);
```

To understand why the two outputs are not the same, consider the *statements* written above: n++; and ++n;. As statements, they simply say "Take the value of n, add 1 to it, *and do nothing else*." Hence, the net result is the same either way. In the experiment, we did not use the *statements* `b++;` and `++a;`. We did, however, require the values returned by the *expressions* `b++` and `++a`. From the first output, it is clear that the original value of `b` is returned. We conclude that `b` gets incremented afterward. From the second output, we see that the original value of `a`, plus `1`, gets returned. Hence we conclude that `a` is incremented first. In general, when the increment operator is a prefix, the value of the variable is not returned until it is incremented. However, when the increment operator is a suffix, the value of the variable is returned prior to incrementing it.

There is another unary operator, `--`, called the *decrement operator*. The discussions above apply to it, except that the operation is to subtract `1` from a variable, not add `1`.

Exercises

(10-1) Given the declarations below, find the value of the expressions that follow:

```
int a = 2, b = 4, c = 3, d = 1, e = 2;

(a)  (a++) - (++b)
(b)  (++a / ++c) * (c++ / a++)
(c)  (--b) * (c--) - (--d)
(d)  b = (e += 2)
(e)  a %= (--b)
```

10.3

MACROS

A *macro* is essentially an abbreviation. We have already seen a very simple *C* language macro: the symbolic constant. Recall that when the *C* preprocessor encounters the name of a symbolic constant, it replaces the name with the value given in the `#define` statement. In *C*, we can use `#define` to name an expression that contains one or more variables. Consider the following:

```
#define  VOLUME(n)  3.14 * (n) * (n) * (n) * 4.0/3.0
```

This is the definition of a macro used for calculating the volume of a sphere of radius `n`. Although it looks more complicated than a constant definition, the idea is the same: the keyword `#define`, followed by an identifier `VOLUME(n)`, followed by the replacement text `3.14*(n)*(n)*(n)*4.0/3.0`. In the body of a program, we might very well use the `VOLUME` macro like this:

```
   ...
z = VOLUME(x);
   ...
```

The preprocessor replaces every invocation of `VOLUME(x)` by `3.14*(x)*(x)*(x)`
`*4.0/3.0`, so the above code is compiled as if it were written like this:

```
   ...
   z = 3.14 * (x) * (x) * (x) * 4.0/3.0;
   ...
```

It may appear that we have gone overboard with our use of parentheses. The next experiment shows that this is not the case.

EXPERIMENT 10-2

(a) Define `VOLUME(x)` as above, except don't include parentheses around the `x`'s on the right side. Write a program that calculates a volume like this:

```
   m = 4;
   vol = VOLUME(m);
```

(b) Repeat the above, only change `VOLUME(m)` to `VOLUME(m+2)`. What value is actually calculated? Explain.

Exercises

(**10-2**) Consider each of the following macro definitions:

```
#define   cost(n)    3 * (n) + 7
#define   temp(n)    1.8 * (n) + 32
#define   perimeter(n,m)   2 * (n) + 2 * (m)
```

Write the replacement code for each of these calls:

```
cost(x + b)
temp(x + b)
perimeter(n + b, m + b)
```

What values are returned if `x = 2`, `m = 4`, and `n = -1`?

(**10-3**) Repeat the previous exercise, but assume that the replacement code in each macro definition lacks parentheses.

10.4

COMPILATION SCHEMES

Up to this point, we have been compiling our programs without thinking very much about the compilation step. We simply invoke the compiler (or perhaps just give the system a command like RUN) and leave it at that. In this section, we will look at two options regarding compilation:

- It is possible to give the computer a choice in the way it compiles a particular program, and base that choice on certain conditions. This is known as *conditional compilation*.
- It is possible to split a program into several files and compile the files separately. That idea, called *separate compilation*, is useful when dealing with large programs where not every file needs to be recompiled during the debugging process.

10.4.1 Conditional Compilation

We have so far seen two important preprocessor statements: `#include` and `#define`. There is a third one that instructs the preprocessor to compile a section of a program only if a given condition obtains[2]:

```
#if <constant expression>
    <program lines>
#endif
```

If the value of `<constant expression>` is nonzero, then the code symbolized by `<program lines>` compiles. Otherwise, those lines don't compile. For example, suppose our computer has unique features that can be exploited by a set of customized commands that would be meaningless if executed on any other computer. We can define a constant called **FEATURE** whose value is either `1` (if the computer has the features) or something other than `1` (if the computer does not have the features). In every place in the program where one of these custom commands comes up, we surround those lines with the above `#if-#endif` keywords:

```
#if FEATURE == 1
    <lines with customized commands>
#endif
```

If **FEATURE** is `1`, the lines representing the customized commands compile. Otherwise, the compiler ignores them.

There is an `#else` option to this preprocessor statement that enables the preprocessor to choose between two alternatives:

```
#if FEATURE == 1
    <custom command set 1>
#else
    <custom command set 2>
#endif
```

---

2 Don't confuse this with the `if-else` statement; this is a message to the preprocessor.

If the value of expression **FEATURE == 1** is nonzero, the first set of program lines compiles. Otherwise, the second set compiles.

Program 10.1 illustrates conditional compilation. On a certain compiler, Program 7.1 will not compile as it is written. In particular, the function **assign_values** must be modified as follows:

```
scanf("%f %d", &(pt->price), &(pt->doors));
```

should be replaced by

```
scanf("%f %d", &dummy, &(pt->doors));
pt->price = dummy;
```

It is assumed that **dummy** is declared locally as **float**. Since we do not know in advance which compiler will be used, we can put both versions of the function in our program (line [2]).

```
#if PROBLEM == 1
        <version 1 of function>
#else
        <version 2 of function>
#endif
```

The constant **PROBLEM** is defined to be 1 if the offending compiler is used. For other compilers, **PROBLEM** would be changed to, say, 0.

Exercises

(10-4) It is illegal to nest comments. Suppose we wish to comment out a large section of code that already has comments in it. How would we use conditional compilation to accomplish this task?

(10-5) How would we use conditional compilation to choose between two different versions of an **include** file?

10.4.2 Separate Compilation

As indicated above, we can divide a program into more than one file, then compile the files separately. This enables us to concentrate on the part of a program that might need extra attention, while avoiding unnecessary recompilation of the remaining (presumably satisfactory) parts. The main issue in separate compilation is how the compiler can recognize identifiers that are needed throughout the program (i.e., in several of the files) but defined in only one of them. The best way to understand this is to look at a very simple example that illustrates the basic ideas. Consider the following two files, `mod1.c` and `mod2.c`:

```
#include<stdio.h>          /* this is mod1.c */
main()
 {
   void          fun(int);
   extern  int   m;
   fun(m);
   printf("bye bye \n");
 }
```

and:

```
#include<stdio.h>          /* this is mod2.c */
static int   k = 10;
int          m = 50;

void fun(int i)
 {
   printf("%d \n", k + 3 * i);
 }
```

Let's start with the function `fun`. This is defined in `mod2.c`, so when `mod2.c` is compiled, the compiler has no problem with it. Note that a prototype is not needed here, since the definition of `fun` itself is the compiler's first encounter with it. However, `fun` is called in `mod1.c`. Therefore, a function prototype for `fun` appears in `mod1.c` so that the compiler can deal properly with the function call.

What about the variables `m` and `k`? These are defined in `mod2.c` prior to the function, so they are both global to that function. However, `k` is not known throughout the program. The keyword **static** has the effect of making `k` private to `mod2.c`. If a function had been defined in `mod1.c`, then that function would not be able to access `k`. The variable `m`, on the other hand, is accessible from both the main program, in `mod1.c`, and the function `fun`, in `mod2.c` (since `m` is global to that function). The keyword **extern** in the declaration in `mod1.c` is essentially a promise to the compiler that although `m` is not defined there, it is defined in another module. Eventually the compiler will find out what it needs to know about `m`. Without **extern**, the compiler would consider `m` an unknown identifier.

Finally, we have the variable `i`. This should be no mystery: It is not only unknown outside `mod2.c`, it is unknown outside `fun`.

EXPERIMENT 10-3

To gain familiarity with the logistics of separate compilation, compile `mod1.c` and `mod2.c` separately. Then link them together and run them. Now completely remove the definition of `m` in `mod2.c`. Can this be compiled successfully? How about linking? Explain the result.

Exercise

(10-6) Consider a program `mod1.c` that calls two functions, `fun1` and `fun2`. Each function takes an integer as input, and returns an integer as output. The functions are compiled in `mod2.c`. Write three program skeletons—one for each situation listed below—showing declarations and definitions needed for the two modules.

> **(a)** Variable `g1` is passed to `fun1`, and variable `g2` is passed to `fun2`.
>
> **(b)** Both `g1` and `g2` must be unknown outside `mod1.c`.
>
> **(c)** A variable `g1` is defined in `mod2.c` and passed to `fun1`.

10.5

TWO UNUSUAL OPERATIONS

In this section, we look at the so-called *comma operator*. To appreciate this operator, which allows us to use a pair of expressions in place of a single one, we will need to see some examples. We will also look at another way (in addition to `if` and `switch`) for a program to make choices.

The Comma Operator

In *C*, we can create a new expression (called a *comma expression*) by writing several unrelated expressions separated by commas:

```
<expression 1> , <expression 2> , ... <expression n>
```

The value of the entire comma expression is the same as the value of the last expression in the sequence. The values of the foregoing ones are ignored.

The obvious question is, *why bother*? If the values of the first $n-1$ expressions are ignored, why not just use the n-th expression by itself? The answer is a bit subtle. Back in Chapter 1, when we were just beginning, we usually pictured expressions as objects like these:

```
x * ( y - 6);
x - y + 2 * (z + 4);
```

Now that we have more exposure to *C*, we can appreciate that the world of expressions is rather large. For example, function calls without the semicolon at the end are expressions.[3] The following example illustrates an interesting use of this fact:

Example: Comma Operator

```
if ( scanf("%d", &x), x > 10 )
    printf("This is pretty neat. \n");
```

---

3 Remember, a statement is technically an expression followed by a semicolon!

Note that the conditional expression of the `if` statement is a comma expression. Here, the `scanf` function is executed, and the value of the expression `x > 10` is taken to be the value of the `if` condition. In effect, we have killed two birds with one stone: An input value has been read, and we have provided a terminating condition for the `if` statement. In general, the idea is to use all but the last expressions of a comma expression for any actions they might produce (rather than the values that they have), and use the last expression for its value. Remember, a comma expression, no matter how complicated, is an *expression*, not a statement. It can be used in any situation that calls for an expression.

Very interesting applications of the comma expression involve its use in `for` loops.

Example: Comma Operator

```
for (n = 1; n <= 10; printf("%d \n", n*n), n++);
```

Here, the increment rule is a comma expression. The last part, `n++`, is the only part that gets evaluated, so the `for` loop has a normal increment rule. The first part of the comma expression does not control the loop at all; it is there simply to output numbers. The net result is that we have created a `for` loop that prints out the squares of the first ten integers, yet has no body!

Exercises

(10-7) Explain the action of each of these statements:

```
(a)    if (scanf("%d %d", &x, &y), x < y)
           printf("hello \n");

(b)    for (scanf("%d", &x), n = 0; n <= x; n++)
           printf("hello \n");

(c)    while (a = 1, x = 3, y = 2, n > 0)
           {
              x--;
              y--;
              n = x + y;
              printf("hello \n");
           }

(d)    printf("%d is the answer \n", printf("hello \n"), z);
```

(10-8) Rewrite each of the above exercises without the comma operator.

Conditional Expressions

A *conditional expression* is composed of three expressions, separated by a question mark and a colon, as follows:

```
<expr 1> ? <expr 2> : <expr 3>
```

The computer makes a choice between `<expr 2>` and `<expr 3>` based on the value of `<expr 1>`:

- If `<expr 1>` ≠ 0: `<expr 2>` is evaluated.
- If `<expr 1>` = 0: `<expr 3>` is evaluated.

Furthermore, the choice that is ultimately made becomes the value of the entire expression.

Example: Conditional Expressions

```
(1)    time   =   hour > 12 ? hour - 12 : hour;

(2)    printf("The lower fee is %f. \n", x < y ? x : y);

(3)    printf(x == y ? "Score tied.\n" : "Game over.\n");
```

The first example converts 24 hour time to 12 hour time, assigning to `time` one of the two expressions `hour  -  12` or `hour` as appropriate. In the second example, if `x` is the lower rate, `x  <  y` evaluates to 1, and the value of `x` is printed. Otherwise, the value of `y` is printed. In the last example, one of two strings is printed.

EXPERIMENT 10-4

(a) With a conditional *statement*, one can leave out the `else` part. What happens if we leave out the expression that follows the `:` in a conditional *expression*?

(b) Can a comma expression be used in either part of a conditional expression?

It should be understand that a conditional expression is not the same thing as a conditional statement. A conditional expression is an *expression*; it is used wherever an expression can be used. A conditional *statement* cannot be used where an expression is required. There are two additional differences:

- A conditional statement can have rather complex compound statements in each part. It is impossible for a conditional expression to substitute for this.
- A conditional expression must have an `else` part; a conditional statement need not have one.

Exercises

(10-9) Describe the action of each of these conditional expressions:

```
(a)    y = 2 * (n > 0 ? y + 2 : y - 2);

(b)    for (n = 0; a < b ? n < b : n < a; n++)
           printf("hello \n");

(c)    scanf("%d", a < b ? &a : &b);
```

(10-10) Rewrite each of the above without using conditional expressions.

(10-11) Evaluate the following statement for x = 2 and for x = 1:

```
if (x == 2 ? x - 2 : x)
    printf("hello \n");
```

(10-12) If possible, write each of the following statements without any **if**.

```
(a)  if (a == b)
         printf("hello \n");
     else printf("goodbye \n");

(b)  if (m < n)
         x = 10;

(c)  if (m < n)
         printf("hello \n);

(d)  if (m > n);
         else printf("hello \n");
```

10.6

PASSING PARAMETERS TO main

Some operating systems allow for parameters to be passed to **main**. The logistics of this are as follows: When the command to run the program is issued, the parameters to be passed are typed in following the command, separated by spaces.[4] For example, the MS-DOS **diskcopy** command might be written like this:

```
C:\> diskcopy a: b:
```

Here, c:\> is assumed to be the command line prompt. The parameters a: and b: are passed to the main program, **diskcopy**.

---

4 These are sometimes called *command line arguments*.

The mechanism for passing parameters to `main` is quite unusual. No matter how many arguments are to be passed to `main`, it is declared with only two formal parameters:

- An integer.
- An array of pointers, each of which points to a string.

Programmers frequently name these two parameters `argc` and `argv`, respectively, though this is not absolutely necessary. As long as the data types are as indicated, the declaration will work. The following is typical of the declaration of `main` in the case where command line arguments are to be passed:

```
main(int  argc, char  *argv[])
```

When the program name is invoked, along with the command line parameters, the total number of parameters, plus 1, is stored in `argc`. The name of the program is stored in `argv[0]`, and the command line parameters are stored from `argv[1]` on, in the order in which they are typed. The programmer accesses the parameters in those locations, and deals with them as appropriate. For the `diskcopy` example above:

```
argc = 3
argv[0] = "diskcopy"
argv[1] = "a:"
argv[2] = "b:"
```

Exercise

(10-13) In each case below, assume that the first string after the prompt is the name of a program to be run. Also assume that the remaining strings are parameters to be passed to **main()**. All strings are separated by spaces. Completely describe **argc** and **argv** in each case:

```
(a)  remove ints.dat /e
(b)  copy file.one  b:file.two
(c)  move file.one b:
(d)  filelist
```

10.7

VARIABLE-LENGTH PARAMETER LISTS

Up to now, every function that we have defined has conformed to the following idea: The number of actual parameters in a function call must be the same as the number of formal parameters in a function definition. This means that the number of parameters we can pass is fixed at the time we define the function. An alert reader may have already noted that two important functions—**printf** and **scanf**—do not seem to suffer from this restriction. In this section, we will answer a simple question: *How is that possible?* For convenience, we will refer to functions such as `printf` and `scanf` as *variable argument* functions. We will provide a means for defining a function so that it can be called with an arbitrary number of parameters. This is a pretty advanced topic for an introductory book, so we will proceed slowly. First we will give a somewhat sketchy overview. Then we will fill in the details.

Overview

In order to work properly, a variable argument function needs two things:

1. A way to determine the number of parameters passed in a given call.
2. A method of accessing each of the parameters.

With a little thought about `printf`, we can figure out the first item above. Every `printf` has one required parameter: the control string. The other parameters are optional (though they are almost always present). Recall that a control string contains zero or more format specifiers. Since each format specifier represents an optional parameter, the control string indirectly gives the total number of optional parameters. The programmer of the `printf` function simply counts the number of format specifiers, and knows how many parameters are passed for any given call. In general, a variable argument function must be defined with at least one *required* parameter: one that tells the function how many optional parameters there are.

As for accessing the parameters, the basic ideas are as follows: The parameters of a given call are put on a list, with the optional ones following the required ones (Figure 10.1). The parameters are accessed by moving a pointer sequentially from the first optional parameter to the last. This must be done according to the following conventions:

1. Declare the pointer.

2. Invoke a macro[5] to point to the first optional parameter.

3. Invoke a second macro to retrieve the value of the parameter pointed to. Do this for each optional parameter.

4. Invoke a third macro to terminate the process after all optional parameters have been accessed.

The header of a variable argument function has this general form:

```
<return type>    <name>(<required parameter list>, ...)
```

---

5 The macros for these operations are found in a header file called `stdarg.h`. This file must be included when variable argument functions are used.

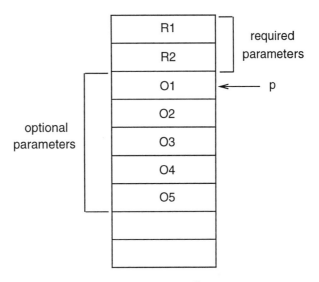

Figure 10.1 Schematic diagram of variable length parameter list.

Note that the three dots are to be taken literally. They signify that optional parameters may be passed. Here is an example:

```
int     sumsq(int  x, ...)
```

Thus the function **sumsq** may be called with one or more paramters. The first parameter *must* be an integer.

Details

In Program 10.2 we have written a function that adds the squares of a list of integers input to it. The prototype for this function is shown in line [1] of the program. It consists of the type name **int**, followed by the three dots. Except for the function name, the prototypes of all variable argument functions look the same. Here is the implementation of the four steps listed above:

1. We call the pointer to the arguments **argp** (line [2]). In **stdarg.h**, the special type name **va_list** is given to a pointer designed to point to the list of optional parameters. Hence, we must declare **argp** with this type name:

```
va_list     argp;
```

2. We use a macro called **va_start** which points **argp** to the first optional parameter (line [3]):

```
va_start(argp, n);
```

The first argument to **va_start** is the pointer name; the second is the name of the last required parameter. Since the first optional parameter follows the last required one, pointing to the latter enables the computer to find the former.

3. We retrieve the value of the parameter pointed to by `argp` using a macro called `va_arg` (line [4]):

```
z = va_arg(argp, int);
```

Here `z` has been declared as type `int`. The first argument is the pointer name; the second is the data type of the value returned by the call. `va_arg` returns the value of the parameter pointed to by `argp`, then moves `argp` so that it points to the next parameter on the list.

4. After all parameters have been accessed, it is necessary to terminate the process using the macro `va_end` (line [5]):

```
va_end(argp);
```

EXPERIMENT 10-5

(a) From the descriptions above, it is clear that we cannot access the arguments of a variable argument function without `va_start` and `va_arg`. But what about `va_end`? This comes *after* we have accessed everything. Is it a serious mistake to leave it out? (This is a hard question to answer. Let's define serious as bad enough to be caught by the compiler.) Will the compiler stop us from not using it?

(b) Run Program 10.2 with the first (required) parameter changed to `5`, and everything else left the same. Explain what happened.

(c) Now run Program 10.2 with the first (required) parameter changed to `15`, and everything else left the same. Use your knowledge of arrays to explain what happened.

Exercises

(10-14) Write the headers for multiple argument functions that take the input parameters indicated:

(a) A string, plus any number of integers.

(b) At least four integers.

(c) At least four floating point numbers.

(d) Any number of floating point numbers.

(10-15) All the examples and exercises in this section have dealt with variable-length parameter lists whose parameters have the same data type. What if the parameters on the variable-length list have different data types? What would the header of the function look like? (Hint: Think about how `printf` and `scanf` work. What must each of those functions have at a minimum?)

Programming Problems

(10-P1) Write a function that accepts any number of arguments of type `int`, `float`, or `char`, then prints out the largest `int`, the largest `float`, and the `char` that is closest to `z` in the alphabet. Test the function by writing a program that calls it with a variety of parameters. (Again, think about `scanf` and `printf`, and the parameters they require at a minimum.)

User Input: None. The parameters to the function are coded into the program.

Program Output: A statement indicating the largest values as described above.

(10-P2) A certain research analyst makes frequent use of trigonometric, logarithmic, and exponential functions in her work. In particular, she often needs a weighted average of two of these functions:

```
avg = w(1)f(x)  +  w(2)g(x)
```

where `w(1)` and `w(2)` are values between 0 and 1 such that their sum is 1. Write a function that returns the value of `avg` if it is passed both weights and both functions. Test this function by writing a program that calls it with a variety of parameters.

User Input: None. The parameters to the function are coded into the program.

Program Output: A statement indicating the value of `avg`.

(10-P3) Write a program that reads a file of 100 integers, then finds the highest and lowest values. Do this by compiling three modules separately: one that reads in all the input and output, one that calculates the highest value, and one that calculates the lowest value.

User Input: A file name.

Program Output: A statement inidicating the largest and smallest values as described above.

PROGRAMS FOR CHAPTER TEN

Program 10.1: Conditional Compilation

```
#include<stdlib.h>
#include<stdio.h>
#include<string.h>
#define PROBLEM 1
```

```
struct vehicle
  {
    char            name[15];
    char            ident[10];
    float           price;
    int             doors;
    struct vehicle  *next;
  };

typedef struct vehicle NODE;
void print_list(NODE *);
void assign_values(NODE *);
void create_header(NODE *);

main()
{
 NODE    *p, *q, *start;
 int     sentinel = 1;

 start = (NODE *)malloc(sizeof(NODE));
 create_header(start);
 p = start;

 while (sentinel != 0)
  {
    q = p;
    p = (NODE *)malloc(sizeof(NODE));
    assign_values(p);
    q->next = p;
    printf("More entries?  [0 to end, 1 to continue]...\n");
    scanf("%d", &sentinel);
  }

 p->next = NULL;
 print_list(start);

void    create_header(NODE *ptr)
  {
    strncpy(ptr->name, "CarList", 7);
    strncpy(ptr->ident, "Head", 1);
    ptr->price = 0.0;
    ptr->doors = 0;
  }

#if PROBLEM == 1
void assign_values(NODE *pt)
{
float   dummy;

printf("Enter name and ID. \n");
scanf("%s %s", &(pt->name), &(pt->ident));
printf("Enter price and number of doors. \n");
scanf("%f %d", &dummy, &(pt->doors));
pt->price = dummy;
}
```

```
#else

void assign_values(NODE *pt)
{
printf("Enter name and ID. \n");
scanf("%s %s", &(pt->name), &(pt->ident));
printf("Enter price and number of doors. \n");
scanf("%f %d", &(pt->price), &(pt->doors));
}
#endif

void print_list(NODE *pt)
{
 while (pt != NULL)

  {
   printf("%s \n", pt->name);
   pt = pt->next;
  }
}
```

Program 10.2: Variable Argument Parameter List

```
      #include<stdio.h>
      #include<stdarg.h>
      main()
       {
[1]    int  sumsq(int, ...);
       int  sum_of_squares;
       sum_of_squares = sumsq(7, 3, 5, 10, 6, 2, 8);
       printf("The sum of the squares is  %d \n", sum_of_squares);
       }

       int    sumsq(int n, ...)         /* n = number of parameters */
        {
[2]      va_list   argp;                /* declare argp */
         int       count, sum = 0;
         int       temp;

[3]      va_start(argp, n);

         for (count = 0; count < n; count++)
           {
[4]          temp = va_arg(argp,int);
             sum = sum + temp * temp;
           }
[5]      va_end(argp);
         return(sum);
        }
```

A

Discussion of Experiments

Experiment 1-1

Depending on the error, the compiler may not pinpoint a syntax error at the exact spot in the source code. However, it will be close enough so that with a little thought, the error can be found and corrected. An error such as `car = 30` instead of `cars = 30` is clear: the compiler doesn't recognize the identifier `car`, since it was not declared. The line `CAR_RATE / 0` is acceptable to the compiler; the syntax is fine. However, the program cannot run properly because it is against the rules of arithmetic to divide by zero. Here, the error occurs when the program runs, not when it compiles. This type of error is called a *run-time error*. (Think of the statement *I will jump off the roof.* It is perfectly good English; it obeys the rules for constructing English statements. However, it is not a statement one would want to put into action!)

Experiment 1-2

There is nothing wrong with `cars=30`. The compiler can figure out that the identifier `cars` ends with the letter "s," and that the `=` is the assignment operator. However, without a space after the `int`, the term `intcars` is treated as a single identifier. Since it is undeclared, the compiler reports an error. In general, spaces are needed between two quantities if the absence of a space makes the two look like a single indentifier.

Experiment 2-1

Test Program:

```
#include<stdio.h>
main()
{
  printf("Real with integer format:   %d \n", 3.14);  /* part a */
```

```
printf("Integer with char format:    %c \n", 3);     /* part b */
printf("Integer with float format:   %f \n", 3);

printf("Character with integer format: %d \n", 'A');  /* part c */

printf("Addition of integer to character:  %c \n", 'A' + 7);
        /* part d */
printf("Also addition of integer to character:  %d  \n", 'A' + 7);
}
```

(a) The compiler does not stop you, but the results are meaningless.

(b) Same as (a).

(c) Gives 65. This is the ASCII value of the character.

(d) Internally, characters are represented as integers. Adding 7 to 'A' gives 72. Printed as a character, this is the value ('H') that is seven characters from 'A'. As an integer, we get $65 + 7 = 72$.

(e) Recall the description of `printf`: "the control string is essentially what gets printed out." If the string has spaces between the format specifiers, then those spaces are simply treated as part of the string, and they will get printed out. If there are no spaces between them, the outputs will be squeezed together.

Experiment 2-2

```
#include<stdio.h>
main()
{
 printf("Addition first:  %d \n", 8 + 4 * 2);
        /* part a */
 printf("Multiplication first:  %d \n", 8 * 4 + 2);

 printf("Division, then multiplication: %d \n", 8 / 4 * 2);
        /* part b-1 */
 printf("Multiplication, then division: %d \n", 8 * 4 / 2);

 printf("Mod, then subtraction:  %d  \n", 8 % 4 - 2);
        /* part b-2 */
 printf("Subtraction, then mod:  %d  \n", 8 - 4 % 2);

 printf("Division, then addition: %d \n", 8 / 4 + 2);
        /* part b-3 */
 printf("Addition, then addition: %d \n", 8 + 4 / 2);
}
```

(b1) In both cases, the answers obtained when the operations are done left to right are correct. Hence, the operators have equal precedence.

(b2) The answer to `8 - 4 % 2` would be `0` if the operations were done left to right. However, the result is actually `8`. Hence, the operations did *not* proceed left to right, and the "`%`" operator has a higher precedence than the "`-`" operator.

(b3) If the operations proceeded from left to right, the answer to 8 + 4 / 2 would be 6, not 10. Hence, / has higher precedence than +.

You can experiment with any pair of operators in this fashion to determine which operator has a higher precedence.

Experiment 2-3

```
#include<stdio.h>
main()
{
  int    x = 3, y = 5;
  float  a = -368.555;

  printf("%1d %1d \n", x, y);                /* part a */
  printf("%2d %2d \n", x, y);
  printf("%10d %10d \n", x, y);

  printf("%f \n", a);                        /* part b */
  printf("%10.2f \n", a);


  printf("%2f \n", a);                       /* part c */
}
```

(a) The output from all three **printf** statements is the same numerically, but the appearances are different. The number just after the percent symbol specifies a *field width* in which the output is right justified.

(b) The output is right justified in a field of 10 characters, and there are two places to the right of the decimal point. In general, **%A.Bf** results in a field width of A characters, with B places to the right of the decimal point.

(c) Leaving off the **.B** in **%A.B** results in the specification being ignored. Instead, the default values of field width and decimal places are used.

Experiment 2-4

```
#include<stdio.h>
main()
{
  int    x, y;
  char   ch1, ch2;
  float  a,b;

  a = 5;                   /*  (1) integer assigned to real */
  printf("%f \n", a);

  x = 5.5;                 /*  (2) real assigned to integer */
  printf("%d \n", x);
```

```
ch1 = 75.5;                 /*  (3)  real assigned to character */
printf("%c \n", ch1);

b = 'J';                    /*  (4)  character assigned to real */
printf("%f \n", b);

y = 'J';                    /*  (5)  character assigned to integer */
printf("%d \n", y);

ch2 = 75;                   /*  (6)  integer assigned to character */
printf("%c \n", ch2);
}
```

The compiler does not stop you in any of the cases.

1. An integer can reasonably be assigned to a floating point number, since the latter includes the former. The compiler casts the **5** into a floating point number before the assignment.

2. It is not logical to assign a real to an integer. The system assigns the integer part of the real to **x**.

3. The ASCII character corresponding to the integer part of the real is assigned to **ch1**.

4. The integer corresponding to the ASCII code for the character is cast into floating point format, then assigned to **b**.

5. The integer corresponding to the ASCII code for the character is assigned to **y**.

6. The ASCII character corresponding to the integer is assigned to **ch2**.

Experiment 2-5

```
#include<stdio.h>
main()
{
  int    a, b;

  printf("Enter 63  54 as one line of input \n");
  scanf("%d", &a);
  printf("%d  \n", a);
  scanf("%d", &b);
  printf("%d \n", b);
}
```

By entering the 63 and 54 on the same line, you are putting two integers into the keyboard buffer. The first **scanf** leaves the internal tracking mechanism immediately following the 63. When the second **scanf** is encountered, the system doesn't have to wait, since there is already an integer in the buffer.

Experiment 2-6

```
#include<stdio.h>
main()
{
  int    a;

  printf("Enter the value 537J \n");

  scanf("%d  \n", &a);
  printf("%d \n", a);
}
```

The J is the first illegal character; the computer regards the 7 as the last digit to read for the integer, and reads the 537.

Experiment 2-7

```
/* Run three times. Enter 8J, 8 J (one space) or 8 J
      (more than one space) */

#include<stdio.h>
main()
{
  int    i;
  char   ch;

  scanf("%d  %c", &i, &ch);
  printf("%d  %c \n", i, ch);
}
```

(a) With the input in this order, any number of spaces can separate the integer and the character. The integer is read into i, and the character is read into ch.

```
/* Run three times.  Enter J8 with no spaces, with one space
    before the J, or with at least two spaces before the J */

#include<stdio.h>
main()
{
  int    i;
  char   ch;

  scanf("%c  %d", &ch, &i);
  printf("%c  %d \n", ch, i);
}
```

(b) When the character comes first, leading spaces are *not* ignored! The leading space is taken as the value for ch. Then the system tries to read the J as the integer. This leads to disaster.

```
/* Run this twice. Enter the value 8J (no spaces at all),
or with at least one space before the 8. */

#include<stdio.h>
main()
{
  int     i;
  char    ch;

  scanf("%c  %d", &ch, &i);
  printf("%c  %d \n", ch, i);
}
```

(c) With no spaces before the 8J, the system reads the 8 for ch. This is fine; the character 8 is read. Then it tries to read the J as an integer. This, of course, is disastrous. With one or more spaces before the 8, a space is read for ch. In attempting to read an integer, the system begins with the 8, and immediately runs into the J, indicating that there is only one digit to this integer. Hence, the 8 is assigned to i.

Experiment 3-1

```
#include<stdio.h>
main()
{
  int     temp = 50;

  if (temp = 100)
  printf("We are at the boiling point. \n");
}
```

The value of temp is initially 50, but the effect of leaving out an equals sign is that 100 is assigned to temp in the header of the if statement. Since the if condition evaluates to a nonzero value, the body of the if executes, even though that is not what we intended.

Experiment 3-2

```
#include<stdio.h>
main()
{
  int     y, x = 4;

  if (x > 4)
     if (y > 10)
         printf("Hello. \n");
  else printf("Goodbye. \n");
}

#include<stdio.h>
main()
{
  int     y = 6, x = 6;
```

```
    if (x > 4)
       if (y > 10)
          printf("Hello. \n");
    else printf("Goodbye. \n");
}
```

When **x = 4**, nothing is output, indicating that there is no **else** part to the first **if**. When **x = 6**, the second if executes, but since **y** is not greater than **10**, the word **Hello** will not print. The fact that **Goodbye** does print is further evidence that the **else** belongs to the second **if**. In general, an **else** belongs to the nearest **if** unless something dictates otherwise.

Experiment 3-3

```
#include<stdio.h>
main()
{
  int    a = 4, b = 5, c = 6;

  if (a < b < c)                    /* part a */
     printf("It sure is! \n");

  if (c > b > a)                    /* part b */
     printf("It sure (?) is! \n");
}
```

Here, the operators associate from left to right. (a) The expression **a < b** is evaluated first. Since **a** is less than **b**, the expression **a < b** evaluates to **1**. The resulting expression—**1 < c**—is evaluated. Since **1** is indeed less than **c**, the entire expression evaluates to **1**. So the first **if** works just fine. (b) The second expression is mathematically true. Again, the operators associate left to right. The expression **c > b** (which is true) evaluates to **1**. Then the expression **1 > a** is evaluated. Since **1** is not greater than **4**, the entire expression evaluates to **0**. Hence, the second **if** does not work as expected. Make your comparisons like this:

```
if( (c > b) && (b > a) )
     printf........
```

Experiment 3-4

```
#include<stdio.h>
main()
{  int  y, x = 10;
   switch (x % 10)
     {
       case 1: y = x + 1;
               printf{"hello one \n");
               break;
```

```
    case 2: y = x + 2;
            printf("hello two \n");
            break;
    case 10: printf("This is OK, but pointless. \n");
 };
}
```

(a,b) The above code compiles and runs; so the absence of **default** is certainly legal. Note, too, that it is also legal to have a case value that can never actually occur (10 in this situation).

```
#include<stdio.h>
main()
{
   int  y, x = 7;
   switch (x % 10)
{
        case 1: y = x + 1;
                printf{"Hello one. \n");
                break;
        default:printf("Did the default case execute? \n");
                break;
        case 2: y = x + 2;
                printf("Hello two. \n");
                break;
        case 10: printf("This is OK, but pointless \n");
        };
}
```

(c) There is no choice of 7 here. As the output shows, the **default** case need not come last.

Experiment 3-5

```
#include<stdio.h>
main()
{
 int    n;
 float  m;

 for (n = 0; n < 5; n++)              /* part a */
    { printf("Does this loop execute five times? \n);
      n = n + 1;
    }

 for (m = 0; m < 5; m = m + 0.5)    /* part b */
    printf("Is a floating point counter OK?  \n");

 for (n = 5; n > 0; n--)             /* part c */
    printf("This is the current value of n:  %d \n", n);

 for (n = 0; n < 5; n++);            /* part d */
    printf("Does this loop execute five times? \n);
```

```
for (n = 0; n < 10; n++);
    printf("Hello \n");
}
```

(a) It is legal (but not advisable!) to tamper with the counter in the loop body.

(b) Floating point numbers are allowed as counters.

(c) The `--` indicates that the loop counter is decremented by 1.

(d) Look at the loop this way:

```
for (n = 0; n < 10; n++)
    /* an empty body  */ ;
printf("Hello \n");
```

The loop consists of a header, followed by a body that is empty. Then comes the `printf` statement. The loop repeats the empty statement, then proceeds to the `printf`, which executes only once. The above syntax is fine, but the logic is not what we intended. Accidentally inserting a semicolon after the header can be a costly mistake.

Experiment 3-6

```
#include<stdio.h>
main()
{
  int     counter = 5;

  while (counter < 10);   /*  semicolon shouldn't be there  */
    {
        printf("Does this loop execute five times? \n);
        counter++;
    }
}
```

With the semicolon after the header, we have a loop with an empty body, followed by a compound statement. When `counter` = 5, the empty body is repeated forever. That is to be expected, since there is no statement in the body to change the loop counter. What we intended to be the body—the compound statement—is never executed, unlike the case of the `for`, where the analogous compound statement is executed once.

```
#include<stdio.h>
main()
{
  int     counter = 15;

  while (counter < 10);   /*  semicolon shouldn't be there  */
    {
        printf("Does this loop execute five times? \n);
        counter++;
    }
}
```

With `counter = 15`, the loop is bypassed completely. Of course, the compound statement is not considered part of the loop; it is simply the statement that follows the loop. Hence, it is executed once. In this situation, what we intended to be the body executes only if the loop is never entered!

Experiment 3-7

Almost all floating point numbers are represented in the machine as approximations to their actual values. The quantity `0.1` is a classic example. Internally, it is very close to, but not quite `0.1`. We expect that after ten iterations the loop should stop, but ten times "`0.1`" does not come out to exactly `1.0`. Therefore, the termination condition is never met. This doesn't mean a real can't be used as a control variable. Instead of testing for the equality of two quantitites, use "`<`" as the operator, and check if the difference between them is small enough. For example, consider this:

```
if (counter - 1.0 < 0.01)
      . . . . . . . . . . .
```

Ten times the value of `0.1` may not be exactly equal to `1.0`, but it is close enough so that the difference between the two values is smaller than `0.01`. Thus the loop can terminate.

Experiment 4-1

```
#include<stdio.h>
main()
{
 int   fun(int);    /* function prototype   */

 /* don't need any statements in main() here.  Just want to
    see if the function compiles.  */
}

int   fun(int  x)        /* function definition */
{
  int  z;
  z = x + 5;
  printf("%d is the value of z.  \n", z);
}
```

(a) We will get either a warning or an error (depending on compiler) if we leave out the return statement.

```
#include<stdio.h>
main()
{
 int   fun(int);    /* function prototype   */
 int   a = 4;

 /* function call */
```

```
printf("The value of fun at a = 4 is  %d \n", fun(a));

}

int   fun(int  x)         /* function definition */
{
  int  z;
  z = x + 5;
  return(z);
  printf("%d  is the value of z \n", z);
}
```

(b) The statements of a function are executed until the `return` is encountered. Anything beyond the `return` is ignored. Thus the `printf` in the function didn't execute.

Experiment 4-2

```
#include<stdio.h>
main()
{
  int   fun(int);    /* function prototype  */
  int   a = 4;

  /* function call */

  printf("The value of fun(5) is  %d \n", fun(5));
  printf("The value of fun(3*5) is  %d \n", fun(3*5));
  printf("The value of fun(3*5 + 1) is  %d \n", fun(3*5 + 1));
  printf("The value of fun(3*5 + a) is  %d \n", fun(3*5 + a));
}

int   fun(int  x)         /* function definition */
{
  int  z;
  z = x + 5;
  return(z);
}
```

(a,b) Yes, all these are legal actual parameters. They are all values that can be copied into the temporary locations created when the function executes.

```
#include<stdio.h>
main()
{
  int   fun(int);    /* function prototype  */

  fun(4);  /*  fun used like a statement, not a variable  */
}

int   fun(int  x)         /* function definition */
{
  int  z;
```

```
   z = x + 5;
   return(z);
}
```

(c) This compiles and runs, but the returned value is lost.

```
#include<stdio.h>
main()
{
 int    fun(int);    /* function prototype  */

 printf("The value of fun(4) is %d \n", fun(4));   /*   function call   */
 printf("The value of z is  %f \n", z);
}

int    fun(int  x)          /* function definition */
{
   int  z;
   z = x + 5;
   return(z);
}
```

(d) The first `printf` shows that the function call is fine. However, the variable z exists only while the function is executing. Since the second `printf` occurs after the function finishes, z is no longer defined. Hence, it can't be printed from the main program.

Experiment 4-3

```
#include<stdio.h>
main()
{
   void    p(void);
   int    p = 6;

   printf("%d \n", p);
}

void    p(void)
{
    printf("Hello \n");
}
```

(a) Illegal, not surprisingly. How would the program be able to tell the difference between them?

```
#include<stdio.h>
main()
{
/* Do the two x's refer to the same quantity? */

   void    p(void);
   int    x = 6;
```

```
    printf("Hello from main! \n");
}

void      p()
{
    int x = 6;
    printf("%d \n", x);
}
```

(b) This compiles, so it must be legal. That means the computer can tell the difference between the **x** reserved for the program, and the temporary **x** created for the function.

```
#include<stdio.h>
main()
{
/* Do the two x's refer to the same quantity? */

    void    p(int);
    int     x = 6;

    printf("Hello from main! \n");
}

void      p(int x)
{
    printf("%d \n", x);
}
```

(c) Same result, and reasoning, as for (b).

```
#include<stdio.h>
main()
{
    void    p(int);

    printf("Hello from main! \n");
}

void      p(int p)
{
    printf("%d \n", p);
}
```

(d) Also legal. The computer can distinguish between the function name **p** and the temporary location **p**.

```
#include<stdio.h>
main()
{
    void    p(int);
    void    q(int);

    printf("Hello from main! \n");
}
```

```
void      p(int x)
{
   printf("%d \n", x);
}

void      q(int x)
{
   printf("%d \n", x);
}
```

(e) Legal. The two x identifiers are separate locations; also, they exist at different times.

```
#include<stdio.h>

int    x = 5;

main()        /* Do the two x's refer to the same quantity? */

{
   void    p(void);

   printf("%d \n", x);
   p(x);
}

void       p()
{
   int x = 8;
   printf("%d \n", x);
}
```

(f) A global variable cannot be accessed from inside a function if the function has declared a local variable of the same name. A name can represent only one quantity, and that is the quantity defined within the function.

(g) No. Each variable name is private to its own function.

Experiment 4-4

```
        /* run again with this change:    int x = 5 */

#include<stdio.h>
main()
{
   void    fun(int);

   fun(5);
   fun(5);
   fun(5);
}
```

```
void      fun(int y)
{
   static int x;
   x = x + y;
   printf("%d \n", x);
}
```

The system initializes the variable **x** to **0**. Hence, the first value printed out is **5**. The **x** in the second call to **fun** is the same one as in the first call, except that it starts out with a value of **5**. Hence, after the second call, its value is **10**. By similar reasoning, we can see that after the third call, the value is **15**.

One would think that the initialization of **x** to **5** takes place each time **fun** is called, in which case the output should always be **10**. However, when a local **static** variable is initialized in the declaration, the initialization is carried out only once. So **x** is set to **5** the first time **fun2** is called, but never again. Thus the **x** retains its value from the previous call.

Experiment 4-5

The results are explained in the text, immediately following the statement of the experiment.

Experiment 4-6

The results are explained in the text, immediately following the statement of the experiment.

Experiment 5-1

```
#include<stdio.h>
main()
{
   int   *p;
   char  *q;

   p = q;  /*  Does this work? */
   q = p;  /*  How about this? */
}
```

Your compiler will either warn you that this is suspicious, or forbid you outright.

Experiment 5-2

```
#include<stdio.h>
main()
{
   int   *p, *q;
```

```
    p = 6;                      /* part a: does this compile? */

    printf("%u \n", q);    /* part b */
    q = NULL;
    printf("%u \n", q);
}
```

(a) The result you get can vary. Technically, you are not allowed to assign a nonzero integer to a pointer. The integer you assign could be a place where code critical to the operation of the machine is stored. You would be courting disaster if you overwrote such code. Hopefully, your compiler will catch you.

(b) The value output after the assignment of NULL is 0. Before any assignment is made, the value is not predictable. It depends on how a machine initializes unassigned pointers. Never use a pointer unless it has been initialized.

Experiment 5-3

```
#include<stdio.h>
main()
{
    int   *p;
    float *q;
    char  *r;

    printf("%d  %f  %c  \n", *p, *q, *r);

}
```

A computer will normally set to some default value any variable that has been declared but not initialized. Hence, each of these pointers points *somewhere*. The system simply interprets the values at those locations as an integer, a floating point number, or a character, and outputs accordingly. This underscores the idea that if a pointer p has not been assigned the address of something, then *p is meaningless.

Experiment 5-4

```
#include<stdio.h>
main()
{
 void  calculate_rate(int, int, int, int*);

 calculate_rate(10, 10, 10, 10);
}

void calculate_rate(int x, int y, int z, int *r)
{
   *r = 22.3*x + 22.3*y + 26.1*z;
}
```

It's illegal. Suppose the system passed the address of the constant 10 to the function. Any attempt by a statement to change this —which is the name of the game with pass by reference—would be futile, since a constant can't be changed. Hence, c does not allow passing constants to address parameters.

Experiment 6-1

The quantities `vehicle` and `&vehicle[0]` are the same: each is the the address of the first element of the array. The actual values printed out are not important; the fact that they are equal is.

The values of `*vehicle` and `vehicle[0]` are the same: 10. The data type of `*vehicle` is the element type of the array.

Experiment 6-2

The problem is that `vehicle` is a constant. It can't be changed by an assignment operation.

Experiment 6-3

All the comparison operations are legal. Addition (subtraction) of an integer to (from) a pointer is legal. Subtraction of two pointers is legal. All other operations are illegal.

Experiment 6-4

This is explained in the text immediately following the experiment.

Experiment 6-5

```
#include<stdio.h>
main()
{
  int    x[5]  =  {22,  4,  16,  -9};
  int    y[5]  =  {22,  4,  63,  9,  0,  12};
  printf("%d   %d \n", x[5], y[6]);
}
```

When there are too few initializers in the declaration, the missing ones are initialized to a default value (usually 0). When there are too many, the compiler flags it as an error.

Experiment 6-6

```
#include<stdio.h>
main()
{
    int    x[5] = {22, 4, 16, -9, 12};
    int n = 5;

    printf("%d  \n", x[n]);          /* part a */

    for (n = 0; n < 6; n++)          /* part b */
        x[n] = x[n] + 1;
}
```

(a,b) In each case, the compiler will let you exceed the array bounds! This is because no syntax rules have been violated. Each statement has been constructed according to the rules of the language.

```
#include<stdio.h>
main()
{
    int    x[5] = {22, 4, 16, -9, 12};

    printf("%d  \n", x[5]);
}
```

(c) This time the compiler catches the error.   There is no such object as x[5].

Experiment 6-7

```
#include<stdio.h>
#define N 10
main()
{
    int    x[N];
    printf("Can you do that?  \n");
}
```

(a) Yes you can. Constants are replaced with their values by the preprocessor; this declaration is as good as int x[10].

```
#include<stdio.h>
main()
{
    int    n;
    int    x[n];
    printf("Can you do that?  \n");
}
```

(c) You can't do this. The dimension of the array must be known at compile time.

Experiment 6-8

This is discussed in the text immediately following the experiment itself.

Experiment 6-9

```
#include<stdio.h>
main()
{
    char    x[10];
    x = "melon";
}
```

You get an error because the string name is a constant; it can't be assigned anything.

Experiment 6-10

```
#include<stdio.h>
main()
{
    char    x[] = "hello";
    char    *p = &x;
    float    z = 555555555.5;
    float    *q = &z;

    printf("%s \n", p);
    printf("%s \n", q);
}
```

First, note that the second declaration points **p** to the string *"hello"*, and that the fourth declaration points **q** to the floating point number **z**. Let us carefully consider **printf** with the string format specifier. For one thing, the quantity in the variable list is a pointer. It is assumed to point to a sequence of characters terminated by the null character, which is really a byte of 0s. In the first **printf**, we can see clearly that this is the case. **hello** is obviously a string, and therefore is terminated by the null character. The second case is more interesting. A floating point number is represented internally using, say, six bytes. We picked one that has a byte of 0s somewhere. When we try to print it using the string format, the computer starts at the beginning and prints each byte as if it were an ASCII character. It stops when it gets to the byte of 0s. Of course, the individual bytes of a floating point number are not meant to be interpreted as characters; some of them may be out of range of the standard ASCII set, so that the printed characters are funny looking. The important thing is that the computer regards a string as a pointer to a group of characters terminated by a byte of 0s. It doesn't care what those characters mean, or even if they are part of an actual string.

Experiment 6-11

(a) The quantity `cars[1]` is the second pointer in the three-pointer array `cars`. Since it points to `MITSUBISHI`, that is what gets written out.

(b) The quantity `cars[1]` can also be thought of as an array of characters. The quantity `cars[1][2]` is the third element of that array. Hence, this is the character `T`.

(c) The quantity `cars[1]` is a pointer to an array of characters. Hence `*cars[1]` is the first element of that array: `M`.

(d) The quantity `cars` is a constant pointer. What gets printed out is an address. Its value is not important for this discussion.

(e) Each of these is the address of the first element of the respective string. Compare the values; let the address of the first one be `a`. If the other two addresses are `a+5` and `a+16`, then the three strings are stored back to back.

Experiment 7-1

(a) The output is `8`. The `5` is lost because the pointer originally pointing to it— `p`—was reassigned to a new location by the second invocation of `malloc`.

```
#include<stdio.h>
 main()
 {
     int  *p, *q;    /*  added another pointer  */

     p = (int *)malloc(sizeof(int));
     *p = 5;
     q = (int *)malloc(sizeof(int));
     *q = 8;
     printf("%d  %d\n", *p, *q);
 }
```

(b) You can define another pointer, `q`, which gets the value output by the second invocation of `malloc`. Thus both values, `5` and `8`, are saved. This is not a great idea if you have to save fifty integers, though, since it means defining fifty pointers.

Experiment 7-2

(a) The outputs are: 7,10; 10,10; 7,7. With `p` = `q`, you are abandoning one of the locations. Both pointers point to the same place. The change to `*p` changes what both `p` and `q` point to.

(b) The outputs are: 7,10; 10,10; 7,10. With `*p` = `*q`, the pointers still point to different locations, although both locations have the same value after this assignment. A subsequent change to `*p` does not affect `*q`.

Experiment 7-3

In both cases, the output is 5. The contents of the location pointed to by **p** weren't erased. By "free" we mean that the memory occupied by the 5 is available for allocation at some point in the future.

Experiment 7-4

```
#include<stdlib>
#include<stdio.h>

struct car
  {
    int            doors;
    struct car     *next;
  };

typedef struct car NODE;

main()
{
 NODE    *p, *q, *start;
 int     n;

 start = (NODE *)malloc(sizeof(NODE));
 q = start;
 p = q;
 p->doors = 4;

 for (n = 0; n < 10; n++)
   { p = (NODE *)malloc(sizeof(NODE));
     p->doors = 4;       /* all doors = 4, so there's no 5 */
     q->next = p;
     q = p;
   }

 p->next = NULL;

 p = start;
 while (p->doors != 5)
   { printf("Looking ... \n");
     p = p->next;
   } /* end while */
 printf(" Sorry, not here. \n");
} /* end main */
```

Each time the 5 is not found, the pointer is moved, and the next node is checked. If one doesn't also check for a **NULL** pointer, then when the computer gets to the last node it will read the **NULL** pointer as the next address. At this point, it is not the list that is being searched, but rather some unknown part of the computer that contains garbage. Obviously, this search will not be successful! How it ends, if it does, will depend on the computer.

Experiment 8-1

```
#include<stdio.h>
main()
  {
    FILE   *infile;
    int    number;

    infile =  fopen("test.dat", "r");

    while(!feof(infile) )
      {
        fscanf(infile, "%d", &number);
        printf("Value is %d \n", number);
      }
    fclose(infile);
  }
```

Suppose the 26 has just been read. The value 26 is then printed, and the loop gets ready for the next pass. Since the last read did not detect the end of file, the expression feof is *false*, and the loop can execute again. This time, the end of file *is* detected. However, before the loop finishes the contents of number must be printed. Since number is still 26, another 26 is printed. The next time the loop condition is evaluated, feof is *true*, and the loop halts. With the reverse order of the statements in the body, the end of file is detected immediately after the first 26 is printed. The loop does not have another chance to execute and print the 26 again.

Experiment 8-2

```
#include<stdio.h>
main()
  {
    FILE   *fdes;
    char   ch;

    fdes =  fopen("test.dat", "r");
    fscanf(fdes,  "%c", &ch);

    while(!feof(fdes) )
      {
        printf("Value is %c \n", ch);
        fscanf(fdes, "%c", &ch);
      }
    fclose(fdes);
  }
```

The answer to this problem is quite simple: the `newline` character is treated as a blank by `fscanf`. This is very important. It means that you can't use `fscanf` to determine whether you have reached the end of a line of input, and started the next line.

Experiment 9-1

```
#include<stdio.h>
main()
{
 int  power(int, int);

 printf("The value of %d to the power %d is %d \n", 4, 5, power(4,5));
}

int  power(int x, int y)
{
  if (y==1)
    return(x);
  else return( power(x,y-1) );
}
```

(a) In the above example, the returned value is 4. In general, the returned value is the value of the base.

```
#include<stdio.h>
main()
{
 int  power(int, int);

 printf("The value of %d to the power %d is %d \n", 4, 5, power(4,5));
}

int  power(int x, int y)
{
  if (y==1)
    return(x);
  else return( x*power(x-1,y) );
}
```

(b) This version is a disaster. What makes each call a smaller version of the problem is the reduced value of the exponent. In this version, the exponent is always the same size; so the base case can never be reached.

Experiment 10-1

This is discussed immediately following the experiment.

Experiment 10-2

```
#include<stdio.h>
#define VOLUME(z)   3.14 * z * z * z * 4/3
main()
{    int      m = 4;

     float    vol;

     vol = VOLUME(m);
     printf("The volume is  %f \n", vol);

     vol = VOLUME(m + 2);
     printf("The volume is now %f \n", vol);
}
```

With parentheses, the area for (b) is 904.32. Without parentheses, we get:

```
3.14 * m + 2 * m + 2 * m + 2 * 4/3
```

Since multiplication has a higher precedence than addition, the above problem consists of the sum of four products, plus a 2. The result is 31.23, a far cry from the actual answer. Use parentheses in macro definitions!

Experiment 10-3

No problem in compiling. In mod1.c, the **extern** declaration satisfies the compiler. In mod2.c, the m is not used at all; so removing the definition will not bother the compiler. However, when you try to link, there will be a problem: The promise that m is defined externally has not been met. For the package as a whole, there is no definition of m; the program cannot work.

Experiment 10-4

```
#include<stdio.h>
main()
{
  int x = 5, y = 2, z;

  z = 5 * (x < y ? x + 1 : y - 1) + x;
  printf("%d \n", z);

  z = 5 * (x < y ? x + 1 : ) + x;
  printf("%d \n", z);

  z = 5 * (x < y ? x + 1) + x;
  printf("%d \n", z);
}
```

(a) You get a syntax error in both the second and third calculations of z. There must be two expressions following the question mark.

```
#include<stdio.h>
main()
{
int x = 5, y = 2, z;

z = 5 * (x < y ? printf("hi \n"), x + 1 : printf("bye \n"), y - 1) + x;
printf("%d \n", z);

}
```

(b) Any expression is legal in either part of the conditional expression. If you put a comma expression there, keep in mind that the last one in the sequence is the one that gets evaluated. Otherwise there's no problem.

Experiment 10-5

(a) The compiler does not catch you. You *may* have problems of a subtle nature (translation: you probably won't be able to figure out what's wrong) if you don't use **va_end**. This macro helps the called function to return normally.

(b) Only the numbers 3, 5, 10, and 6 are summed.

(c) The computer looks for eight integers beyond the six you put in. Since they are not there, the results are not predictable.

B

Notes on Some Library Functions

Math Functions (include `math.h` in source code)

cos:

Purpose: To calculate the cosine of an angle θ.

Input: A floating point number θ in radians.

Output: A floating point number: the cosine of θ.

Example: `printf("%f \n", cos(0.79));` prints `0.70`

sin:

Purpose: To calculate the sine of an angle θ.

Input: A floating point number θ in radians.

Output: A floating point number: the sine of θ.

Example: `printf("%f \n", sin(0.8));` prints `0.72`

tan:

Purpose: To calculate the tangent of an angle θ.

Input: A floating point number θ in radians.

Output: A floating point number: the tangent of θ.

Example: `printf("%f \n", tan(0.65));` prints `0.76`.

exp:

Purpose: To calculate the exponential of a number **x**.

Input: A floating point number **x**.

Output: A floating point number: e^x.

Example: `printf("%f \n", exp(-1.29));` prints `0.28`.

log:

Purpose: To calculate the natural logarithm of a number `x`.

Input: A floating point number `x`.

Output: A floating point number: `ln(x)`.

Example: `printf("%f \n", log(2.5));` prints `0.92`.

log10:

Purpose: To calculate the base `10` logarithm of a number `x`.

Input: A floating point number `x`.

Output: A floating point number: `log₁₀(x)`.

Example: `printf("%f \n", log10(2.5));` prints `0.40`.

pow:

Purpose: To compute the power of a number.

Input: A positive number `x`; an integer `y`.

Output: A floating point number: x^y.

Example: `printf("%f \n", pow(3.5, 3));` prints `42.88`.

sqrt:

Purpose: To calculate the non-negative square root of a number `x`.

Input: A floating point number `x`.

Output: A floating point number: $\sqrt{x}$.

Example: `printf("%f \n", sqrt(55));` prints `7.42`.

abs:

Purpose: To calculate the absolute value of a number `x`.

Input: A floating point number `x`.

Output: A floating point number: | x |.

Example: `printf("%f \n", abs(-3));` prints `3`.

rand:

Purpose: To generate a random number.

Input: None.

Output: An integer between 0 and 32767.

Example: `printf("%d \n", rand());` prints an integer between 0 and 32767

String Functions (include `string.h`)

In this discussion

(a) S1 is a string that has been assigned the value "`help`."

(b) S2 is a string that has been assigned value "`less`."

(c) S is a string that has not been initialized.

All three are assumed to be declared as 80 character strings.

`strncpy`:
Purpose: To copy n characters of one string (S2) to another (S1).
Input: S1, followed by S2, followed by n.
Output: Modified S1.
Example: `printf("%s \n", strncpy(S1, S2, 3));` prints `lesp`.

`strcat`:
Purpose: To append one entire string (S2) to another (S1).
Input: S1 followed by S2.
Output: Modified S1.
Example: `printf("%s \n", strcat(S1, S2));` prints `helpless`.

`strncat`:
Purpose: To append up to n characters of one string (S2) to another (S1).
Input: S1, followed by S2, followed by n.
Output: Modified S1.
Example: `printf("%s \n", strncat(S1, S2, 2));` prints `helple`.

`strcmp`:
Purpose: Compares two strings S1 and S2.
Input: S1 followed by S2.
Output: The value S1[i] – S2[i] where i is the index of the first character where S1 and S2 differ.
0 if S1 and S2 are identical.
Example: `printf("%d \n", strcmp(S1, S2));` prints `-4`.

`strncmp`:
Purpose: Compares the first n characters of two strings S1 and S2.
Input: S1, followed by S2, followed by n.

Output: The value S1[i] – S2[i] where i is the index of the first character
where S1 and S2 differ.

0 if the first n characters are identical.

Example: `printf("%d \n", strncmp(S1, "held", 3));` prints 0.

strlen:

Purpose: Find the actual length of a string S.

Input: A string S.

Output: The number of characters in S.

Example: `printf("%d \n", strlen(S1));` prints 4.

gets:

Purpose: Read characters from the keyboard until newline is detected.

Input: A string variable, S.

Output: S, with the keyed in characters assigned to it.

Example: `gets(S);`

If the line "The quick brown fox jumped over the lazy dog." is typed at the keyboard, then s will be assigned that string. The newline character will be replaced by the null character, which becomes the last character of the array s. If there are no characters typed, a null pointer is returned, and s remains unchanged.

fgets:

Purpose: Read characters from a file until newline is detected.

Input: A string variable, s, an integer, n, and a file descriptor, `fdes`.

Output: S, with the keyed in characters assigned to it.

Example: `fgets(S, 80, fdes);`

This statement reads at most 79 characters from the file pointed to by `fdes`, and assigns them to the array s. The newline character is not discarded, as is the case with `gets`. The null character is added to terminate s. If there are no characters in the file, a null pointer is returned, and s remains unchanged.

C

Keywords and Symbols

Symbols used in this text:

;	,	:	=	(	)	{	}	[	]
*	.	#	-	\	'	"	%	&	!
/	+	->	++	--	<	>	<=	>=	==
!=	&&	||	?	+=	-=	*=	/=	%=	

Symbols not used in this text:

~	<<	>>	^	|
>>=	<<=	&=	|=	^=

Keywords used in this text:

auto	break	case	char	default
do	double	else	extern	float
for	if	int	long	return
short	sizeof	static	struct	switch
typedef	union	unsigned	void	while

Other keywords not used in this text:

continue	enum	goto
register	union	

D

ASCII Code

In this chart, we list the *printable* ASCII characters up through ASCII value 126.

32	(space)	56	8	80	P	104	h
33	!	57	9	81	Q	105	i
34	"	58	:	82	R	106	j
35	#	59	;	83	S	107	k
36	$	60	<	84	T	108	l
37	%	61	=	85	U	109	m
38	&	62	>	86	V	110	n
39		63	?	87	W	111	o
40	(	64		88	X	112	p
41	)	65	A	89	Y	113	q
42	*	66	B	90	Z	114	r
43	+	67	C	91	[	115	s
44	,	68	D	92	\	116	t
45	-	69	E	93	]	117	u
46	.	70	F	94	^	118	v
47	/	71	G	95	_	119	w
48	0	72	H	96	`	120	x
49	1	73	I	97	a	121	y
50	2	74	J	98	b	122	z
51	3	75	K	99	c	123	{
52	4	76	L	100	d	124		
53	5	77	M	101	e	125	}
54	6	78	N	102	f	126	~
55	7	79	O	103	g		

E

Precedence Rules

In this table, precedence order for operators we used in this book is listed in groups. An operator in a group that is listed above one in another group has the higher precedence. Two operators in the same group have equal precedence. Association is from left to right *except* for those in the second group, the conditional operator, and the assignment operator.

```
( )         function call
[ ]         array index
.           struct member access
->          struct member access with pointer
------------------------------------------
Right to left associativity for this group:

!           logical NOT
-           negation
++          increment
--          decrement
&           address
*           dereference
(type)      cast
sizeof      size
------------------------------------------
*           multiplication
/           division
%           remainder
------------------------------------------
+           addition
-           subtraction
------------------------------------------
<           less than
>           greater than
<=          less than or equal to
>=          greater than or equal to
------------------------------------------
```

```
==          equality
!=          inequality
---------------------------------------------
&&          logical AND
---------------------------------------------
||          logical OR
---------------------------------------------
Right to left associativity for this:

?:          conditional operator
---------------------------------------------
Right to left associativity for this:

=           assignment
---------------------------------------------
,           comma operator
```

F

Further Reading

For those interested in going further than the basic material in this book, there are many possibilities. "Going further" to me means learning more about the *C* language, learning more about the art and science of programming, and moving on to *C++*. The following small list should help you get started.

- *C How to Program* by Deitel and Deitel (Prentice-Hall): They go into many details about the language not covered in my book.
- *The Art and Science of C* by Roberts (Addison-Wesley): Covers the language more fully and discuses the *whys* of programming quite extensively.
- *The Standard C Library* by Plauger (Prentice-Hall): A reference manual giving the details of the standard *C* library functions.
- *The Object Concept* by Decker and Hirshfield (PWS Publishing): A good introduction to object programming using *C++*.
- *Using Borland C++* by Perry et al. (Que): A huge combination text reference for a popular *C++* implementation.
- *Visual C++* by Andrews (SAMS): Another huge book about another popular system: Microsoft Visual *C++*.

Index